RIDING
AND
TRAINING

HORSEKEEPING

RIDING
AND
TRAINING

Ray Saunders

STERLING
PUBLISHING CO., INC. NEW YORK

Other titles in the **Horsekeeping** *series*
Ownership, Stabling and Feeding
Management: Ailments and Injuries
Small-scale Breeding

Published in the United States and Canada by
Sterling Publishing Co Inc
2 Park Avenue, New York
New York 10016

Produced for the publisher by
MIDAS BOOKS
12 Dene Way, Speldhurst
Tunbridge Wells, Kent TN2 0NX

ISBN 0-8069-3752-1 (Hardcover)

ISBN 0-8069-7068-0 (Paperback)

Printed in Great Britain

Contents

1 Analysing the rider 7

2 Analysing the horse 16

3 Principles of riding and training 24

4 Early training of the young horse or pony 35

5 Lungeing and long-reining 45

6 Elementary schooling 55

7 Learning to jump 67

8 More advanced training 76

9 Gymnastic training 91

10 Training aids and facilities 101

Index 111

Colour plate section between pp.64–65

Acknowledgements

My grateful thanks to my editor, Candida Hunt, who once again has managed to reduce my text to fit the format of the book without any substantial loss of content. My thanks also to Lynne Davey, BHSAI and to Bernard Elliott for helping me demonstrate certain aspects featured in this book.

My photographer, Jack Neal, has also once more worked tirelessly with me to produce the photographs and ensure that each one fits the text of the book. My insistence on each picture being accurate to the split-second necessary to show exactly the part of each movement that I want the reader to see called for painstaking attention to detail and has resulted in an accurate photographic record showing both horse and rider at the crucial moment of each gymnastic movement. This is far superior to drawings, which only give the artist's impression of how he or she thinks it *should* look; many books that rely on drawings give a false impression of what actually happens!

Finally I must mention my wife Jill, who helps out in all departments of the work both with the horses and the production of the series, thus giving me the time to commit it to paper.

Note

Although the author was himself not wearing a hat when the photographs for this book were taken, it is his belief that the wearing of protective headgear is most advisable, not only for the young and inexperienced riders, but for riders of all levels. He would like to point out that he wears full crash-hat protection when riding cross-country courses or riding thoroughbreds at exercise.

1 Analysing the rider

Before embarking on the handling and training of the horse or pony, I should like to deal with the rider. Reading a book will not teach a person to ride well, but it may help a rider to improve if what is written can be clearly understood and is based on sound principles. I do not wish to make every rider conform to a strict outline, nor do I intend to go into all the theories expounded by the experts, which frankly I sometimes find conflicting and confusing. Rather, I shall try to explain what I consider to be the outstanding practical principles and practices that go into making a good rider, and what will help to make a good rider better. My concern is to encourage the young rider to improve not only physically but also in the mental attitude he adopts. This will bring about a greater understanding of the horse and increase the rider's skill and pleasure. I use the term 'young rider' in the sense of people's riding experience and not their actual age, as I shall be dealing not only with those fortunate enough to learn to ride and even to own their own horse or pony in their youth, but also with those who have taken up riding much later in life – indeed, even in old age.

Physique and physical capabilities

There is no doubt that there are born riders, who by their physical and psychological characteristics display a talent for getting the very best out of a horse or pony. Such natural horsemen and horsewomen are, however, comparatively few, and most of us will have to make the best of our physical shortcomings and less gifted equestrian equilibrium by constant training and self-analysis to try and perfect our riding ability. Many will have to make do with something less than a natural riding physique and a mental 'gift'; by a determined application of sound principles within their physical capabilities these people can still become proficient riders, and may even attain a high level. However, really outstanding riders (and horses) are born and not made – as, indeed, are the star performers of any sport or activity. Of course, to reach the top consistent and dedicated training is still required even for gifted sportsmen. There's an old saying that the sign of true talent is when someone can perform what is difficult with apparent ease. But it is also true that practice makes perfect, so those who find that difficult things *are* difficult to begin with may be pleasantly surprised by what determined practice can achieve.

When we talk of a natural figure for riding we can expect to find a fairly slender body of medium height and build with a good length of leg. Most important of the desirable attributes is a pelvic region that is low and fairly narrow, that is to say a pelvis that is comparatively short between its upper (ilium) extremity and the lower (ischium) part, and is reasonably narrow across the top (hips). This will ensure a low centre of gravity and give a stable seat when the upper body is sitting straight and unconstrained. It is this part of the body that receives and transmits the impulses coming from the horse, and the riding controls originate in the small of the rider's back. Many people not possessing this physical configuration find it difficult to transmit their seat control to the horse, and they are also at a particular disadvantage when it comes to absorbing the pulsating movements received from the horse, for example when trying to do a sitting trot. Large buttock muscles will also impair the rider's low centre of gravity, as the pelvis cannot then be properly stabilized deep into the saddle. Fat, too, will greatly interfere with the maintenance of a deep seat with a low centre of gravity, and also blurs the feel flowing upwards from the horse's back. Unlike muscle and bone shape, with which the rider must make the best of what he or she has inherited, fat in this region is something that can be controlled; serious riders who want to develop and enjoy the advantages of a good seat that affords them maximum control over their horse should endeavour to keep this area of their anatomy free from an excessive build-up of fatty tissue. It is no accident that the majority of horsemen who have a real affinity with the horse have slim hips and waists, as exemplified by Western cowboy rodeo riders, Spanish *vaquero* riders and the like.

Second in importance only to the pelvic area is the thigh, which ideally should be well shaped and lean enough on its inner surface to allow it to lie flat, with the rider's thigh bone in the closest possible contact with the saddle. Riders possessing 'round' thighs with a lot of muscle on the inner surface are often advised to push and massage their thighs to alter their shape and mould them into a flatter inner surface. Frankly I feel this is a waste of time, as the shape of the thigh, governed by the amount and disposition of its fibrous makeup, cannot be permanently altered in this way; one is again rather stuck with what has been inherited. However, something can be done in relation to the development of the actual size of the thigh, and exercises used in conjunction with a fitness programme that I shall describe later should not include any that increase the muscular bulk of the thigh region – on the contrary, they should be aimed at slimming and stretching the thigh muscle as much as possible. When turned inwards from the hip joint, a well shaped, lean thigh causes the knee to maintain the correct position on the saddle and opens the buttocks to allow the pelvis to settle deep and firm in the saddle. If the rider then concentrates on this contact with the inner thigh against the saddle and pushes his knee down, the lower leg will be correctly aligned and the ankle will also automatically be pushed down (provided the saddle and stirrups are correctly adjusted). The necessary elasticity of the rider's skeleton through all the joints of the lower body can be achieved once the art of relaxing the muscles rather than tightening or tensing them has been mastered.

The importance of fitness

The fitness of the rider is important in two ways. First, it ensures that he or she is not overweight and carrying large amounts of fat that interfere with the ability to sit on the horse or pony correctly; second, it ensures that he can actively maintain the effort required to control and train a mount. Weight is of course a matter of correct diet and, just as importantly, one's inherited metabolism, which controls the conversion rate of what we eat. Many people with a weight problem do not constantly overeat and yet have real difficulty in keeping their weight down. I do not believe in starvation diets, as the body must have sufficient food of great variety in order to maintain itself in a healthy state, and health is of prime importance, but some people do need to maintain a fairly strict regime if they want to keep their weight down. Apart from those with weight problems because of over-indulgence or inherited tendencies, there are many who will carry some excess weight at certain stages of life. I refer to the extra fat that is seen at puberty, often referred to as puppy fat, and also that which comes with advancing years, called middle-age spread. The former is a natural phase which will right itself if sensible eating and exercise are practised, and the latter can, to some extent, be controlled in the same way. Both are natural phenomena, as can be witnessed if we look at the animal world.

I have found that eating regular, balanced meals, with a mild cutback on quantity after a binge has caused an upsurge in weight, is all that is necessary to keep the weight and shape of the body constant, and would recommend this method to readers. Don't allow your weight to go on increasing through over-indulgence over a period of years and then suddenly decide to do something about it with crash diets that are harmful. If your weight has crept

9

up over a long period it should be allowed to creep down again. If you have let it gradually increase for many years and you are in or approaching middle age, don't expect to regain your former youthful figure completely.

Having regulated our weight to a degree that allows for active riding without interference, we can also increase the fitness of the body in order to ensure that fatigue does not cause a loss of riding stability. Exercise is the obvious answer here, but one should be careful not to include exercises that develop knotty or lumpy muscles. We need supple muscles that can relax, which will enable the rider to 'fit' the horse. Those lucky enough to have such muscles and who also conform to the desired shape outlined above will find the greatest number of horses that will fit them. The importance of not having lumpy muscles lies in the fact that these usually react in somewhat cramped contraction, whereas we are looking for muscles that will lie flat on the surface of the horse and saddle and exert a squeezing action when applied. This is where women and girls have an advantage over men, though fat – the enemy of the riding figure – is likely to be more prevalent in the important parts of the female than in the male. Fat between the muscle and contact with the horse or pony makes control and feel more difficult.

Rider's exercises for suppleness

Supple muscles that are fit and strong are largely developed by the act of riding itself, but we can also improve their performance by stretching and strengthening them with other exercises. Let me say straight away that I do not advocate performing physical exercises while mounted. I often witness this being done with classes of riders all being made to twist and squirm, much to the discomfort of both rider and horse. I believe this form of exercising is useless, and often does more harm than good. It does nothing to improve the rider's control of the animal, nor does it improve his position or contact with the saddle. What is needed is to teach people to sit still, not to fidget about on the horse, and this unnecessary twisting imposes unnatural pressures on the poor animal which only serve to confuse him, to say nothing of the strain on the tack. Exercises to stretch and strengthen the rider's muscles should therefore be carried out away from the horse and practised as a separate part of one's training.

The best type of exercise programme is one that incorporates bending and stretching movements, which encourage the development of a supple waist and back and the lengthening of the muscles and tendon and ligament attachments of the legs. These exercises will be similar to those employed by ballet dancers to stretch the hamstrings and loosen the muscle masses, encouraging blood flow and bringing about a greater and more elastic range of movement to the joints. My own exercise programme, which I have practised religiously since my youth, includes toe touching, arm and trunk circling, sideways stretching with the arms reaching far down the side of the legs, sit ups and leg raises. These and others will keep the body supple and prevent muscle sag. I also include a short routine of hand balancing and agility movements that I have performed for many years as a means of maintaining muscular coordination and reflex action. Individuals can compose their own routines to suit their particular physical capabilities and the time available. What should be avoided is the type of exercise that develops large muscles and excessive strength, which will only be a hindrance when applied to the horse. Weight training can be useful provided it is properly applied to add strength to certain parts that may be in need of initial strengthening. Other useful sports are swimming, which will supple the body and encourage the development of active but relaxed muscles, and skiing, which has no equal for teaching muscular coordination and control with balanced reflex action. Skiing is also the ideal medium for teaching balance with a shifting centre of gravity, which I shall be discussing later in the book. It is very much on a par with riding in this respect, as one has to master the independent control of upper and lower body through a flexible and supple waist. One often sees the same kind of stiffening of the body in a person learning to ski as one witnesses in someone learning to ride. Only when that person has mastered the art of relaxing and allowing the body to go along with the movement of the horse or downhill undulations can he hope to achieve success.

The older rider

I have already mentioned the problem of overweight in the middle aged, and the thickening of the body that often occurs with approaching old age. Those who have always ridden will have adapted to this problem over the years, and although their riding ability will unquestionably have suffered as a consequence they will nevertheless have learned to adjust their style of riding accordingly. This may not leave them in the best form to control and train their horse, but the experience gained from countless hours in the saddle should ensure that their style and riding position still provides a basis for the proper training of the horse. I say 'should ensure' as there are those – and I have seen many – who have ridden badly all their lives, much to the detriment of their horses. For the older person taking up riding for the first time, it is of course important to strive for fitness and a shape not burdened by too much excessive weight; then, with sufficient experience, there is no reason why they should not go on to train their own horse. A word of warning, though, is not to try to do too much too soon. With ageing comes a slowing down of the body's reflexes that no amount of exercise or training will cure – in fact too much training will only make matters worse, as older muscles that are set in their ways will not adapt and readily respond to over-exertion. The body needs longer to recuperate between sessions, and will respond better if given less of a strenuous nature to do, for shorter periods and with longer periods of rest in between. Again I must criticize some schools of instruction where I have witnessed older people being taught to ride or taking improvement courses. The instructors in these cases have completely overlooked the fact that age must be considered, and the limitations of the mature body be taken into account, when asking such pupils to perform certain movements or attain certain 'correct' riding positions. Riders have been asked to adopt and maintain a leg and body position quite alien to their figures and have been repeatedly criticized for not being able to do this. The only result is to tire the rider, bringing about a loosening of the seat and very often his exit from the saddle onto the ground. Giving these riders exercises to perform in the saddle is likewise harmful, as it only serves to cause kinks and twinges to muscles unaccustomed to such antics. This is not to say that as we get older we are all stiff, unsupple and without muscular coordination and cannot improve with practice, but age is a factor that must be considered. There are still ways for the older rider to achieve a good seat and riding control, and they will be explained later.

Balance

The most important single factor for the correct training and control of the horse is without doubt balance. Riders possessing natural balance and physiques that enable them to respond immediately, without conscious effort and with smooth maintenance of balance, to changing centres of gravity are lucky indeed. Many great horsemen have professed never to have taken a lesson in their lives. Most of these riders, although possessing what at first may seem an unorthodox style, were able to achieve their success because of their inborn sense of balance and control. In racing, Lester Piggott was the supreme example of the vital part balance plays in getting the best from a horse. Many others have tried to imitate his style, but without his particular physical characteristics and inborn sense of balance they have never quite matched him. Such was his perfect balance, it was reckoned that his presence on any horse was worth a stone advantage over his rivals. I make the reservation of saying 'was', as although he is still oustandingly good, anyone after about thirty-five years of age, and often younger, begins to lose his natural ability. The inevitable loss

12

of reflex action and the corresponding stiffening of the body through changes in its physiological structure unfortunately happens to all of us.

The part of the body most vital for successful balance is the back. Much has been written about the rider's spine and its importance in the control of the horse through the pressure it exerts on the seat. Great detail is often gone into about the various angles that must be achieved in both forward and backward inclination by the flexion or contraction of various vertebrae. Indeed, some go as far as to give the number of the particular vertebra that should be used for this! Learning to control the lower back, and using it to impart messages via the seat and saddle to the horse's back, is of vital importance if one wishes to ride properly and train an animal. Equally important is to free this area from tension in order to allow the seat to follow the up and down and forward motion of the horse. However, I believe that a too technical analysis of these movements only serves to confuse the rider, so I will confine my explanation to the use of a single term – the small of the back. I am sure readers will understand where I mean. The proper position of the knee and lower leg will be brought about by using one's seat as the base of support and throwing the small of the back forwards. This position should precede every control originating from the small of the back, and will in effect make the rider grow longer from the hip joints downwards and taller from the hips upwards. Never try forcibly to achieve or hold this position, but relax and come to it naturally. If this cannot be done with a little practice something is wrong with the shape of the saddle, the shape of the horse or pony, or the length of stirrups. Once this position has been comfortably achieved (and your comfort will almost inevitably mean that the horse or pony is also comfortable), the upper body will assume the upright posture of the normal seat which facilitates control of the horse in general. In this position you can remain comfortable for the longest time without growing fatigued. It is also the position that most readily allows the rider to contract his muscles smoothly rather than convulsively so that a 'feel' can be developed between horse and rider, which is an essential part of training the horse to accept and respond to the messages of control.

You will have noticed that I have not used the word 'aids' in my explanations. I think the word aid is a misnomer, for we do not aid the horse by the use of our seat, back and legs but instruct him to accept our messages of control and obedience.

The waist

In order to simplify the method of learning to obtain an 'independent' seat and to acquire the feeling of complete harmony with the horse, it is useful to concentrate on the waist, as it is here that one's point of balance divides. From the waist the two extremities of the rider's body – the upper and the lower halves – go their separate ways in order to maintain balance. I hope that the rider still possesses a waist, as obesity is the arch-enemy of balance. Provided the waist is supple enough for the rider to sit upright, with shoulders back and relaxed, one can concentrate on obtaining the independence of seat and lower body that is necessary in order to follow and respond to the movements of the horse while still maintaining perfect balance. The rider must practise until he or she has mastered the art of mentally and physically isolating the waist and using it as a ball-joint between the upper and lower halves of the body. When this has been learned the rider will be able to cling to and follow the horse in its every movement; at the same time he will grow taller out of the waist and maintain the upper body in perfect balance. Once this feeling of separating the lower body from the upper body has been learned, the head and shoulders remain still and level no matter what is going on below the dividing point of the waist. No more will head and shoulders rock from side to side as the horse or pony moves forwards, as is seen with many riders, with disastrous effects on their balance. Once you have learned to isolate the two halves of your body through the medium of a supple waist you will have achieved the greatest single requirement in obtaining an independent seat and true equilibrium.

The hands

The hands, working through the reins, produce essentially a restraining control, as opposed to the driving controls produced by the rider's seat and legs. The hands' influence, working through a whole series of movements from merely squeezing the fingers or relaxing them to the slight withdrawal of the arms when the small of the back is flexed, will give guidance to the horse. They must be yielding and sustaining. When used alone they can bring the horse to a standstill in one way or another, but they will achieve their real purpose of determining pace, gait, direction and carriage only when used in conjunction with the other controls. Their guidance must never become rigid or unfeeling, and although there will be times when a more energetic control must be applied with the hands this should never become fixed in a hard, unyielding struggle or degenerate into a continuous pulling battle with the horse. 'Soft' hands and a firm seat supported by the small of the back go together in providing the rider with perfect hand control. As to the actual position of the hands in holding the reins, I must once again take issue with the practice now taught by some modern schools of riding. It has become fashionable to teach the rider to hold the hands with the wrists bent inwards and the elbows held away from the body. This is wrong. If the hands are turned inwards when they are not exerting influence a hard, cramped position is produced in which the rider will lose the feel of his horse's mouth and eventually kill the feel the horse has in its mouth. The normal position of the hand should be in a straight line with the outside of the forearm, with the fingers bent at the middle joints to form a hollow fist. Passive contact should be kept with the horse's mouth in a straight line through to the rider's elbow, which should lie naturally against his side. The hand will remain soft and steady, and from this position will draw support from the seat and the small of the back. It follows, therefore, that only if the seat is firm and independent can the small of the back be properly flexed and support the hand: the possession of a good or poor hand is usually the direct consequence of a good or poor seat.

2 Analysing the horse

It must be said at the outset that of the thousands of horses selected for training in the various forms of equestrian activity only a very few will prove exceptional enough to go to the top, and it may take several years to discover whether a particular horse has the necessary ability. For example, in dressage and high school performance even an exceptional horse will need many years of work with an expert trainer to reach something approaching perfection. The stallions at the Spanish Riding School in Vienna need three to four years' training before they are ready to perform *haute école*, and the Spanish *rejoneadore* also needs four years to train his stallion to perform its intricate dressage movements in the bullring. It must be remembered, too, that these animals have been specially selected for their potential from among many – possibly as many as hundreds – throughout the selection process. In other activities, racing for example, horses may be trained in rather less time, but for a horse to learn to carry its rider with balance and poise, displaying unconstrained suppleness while peforming intricate gymnastic exercises, one must reckon on years of training rather than months.

Although not many horses will reach the top every horse or pony, no matter how ordinary, will benefit from correct training and will inevitably become a better, more comfortable and obedient ride. All basic training is the same, whether a horse or pony is destined to carry its rider across country as, for example, in hunting, over obstacles in show jumping or through the gymnastic figures of dressage and high school.

A young horse should be allowed to progress slowly, with no more than gentle riding for eighteen months after it reaches four years old. It will not have matured physically until six years old, and severe exertion before it is seven is unwise if its future use and well-being are to be considered. I am well aware that many do not heed this advice, and some animals will appear to stand up to greater physical activity at an earlier age, but it is nevertheless my considered opinion that it is better to wait. Some activities, such as racing, require the immature horse to work hard but this is purely for financial reasons and not to the benefit of the horse. With the high cost of breeding and feeding today it is also a fact that young stock is often disposed of and brought on at an earlier age than used to be the case. However, restraint in the early years will reward you with a horse or pony that will remain fresh and youthful until twenty years of age or even more, and without suffering from many of the joint and ligament problems experienced by animals worked hard before they are ready.

Another point worth remembering is that many horses that look imposing when first seen disappoint in training. They may possess what is considered perfect conformation, but when worked fail to use their good physique in a correspondingly pleasing manner. A perfect-looking exterior can also hide a retractable spirit, and many a horse less favourably endowed physically and with defects in its conformation will nevertheless use itself better and respond freely to its rider's desires. This amiable temperament and willingness to give of its best are most important characteristics if the rider and trainer are not to be consistently frustrated in their efforts to 'make' the horse. If you can find a horse or pony that reacts instantly with a willing desire to please this counts for a great deal; if it occurs in an animal that has good conformation you are very lucky indeed.

Selection

In choosing a horse or pony much will depend upon the purpose for which it is intended to use the animal. I dealt with the general aspects at some length in the first book of the 'Horsekeeping' series, *Ownership, Stabling and Feeding* so I will now go into greater detail on specific points. If we are looking for a horse capable of performing with comparative ease movements of gymnastic exercise, whether in the form of dressage or of jumping, certain types and breeds of animal will be likely to prove more suitable than others. Conformation plays an important part in this, and when serious schooling is to be given one needs to choose a horse that shows a fair amount of verve. I do not mean by this an animal that is 'scatty' and not easily handled, as a calm temperament is the first important feature in any horse that is to be schooled properly. By verve I mean showing energy and vigour in its movement, with an enthusiastic spirit that responds to control. Usually, but not always, certain physical characteristics will give a fair indication of when verve is present. A good sloping shoulder, with well pronounced withers from which a well carried neck of good length extends, are indications of verve, as are long muscular hindquarters and a reasonable length of back. A good wither is also desirable to carry the saddle properly without it slipping forwards and taking the rider's weight with it, thus upsetting balance. If the shoulder has length and slopes forwards from the wither it will also aid in a good saddle and riding position and further guarantee good movement. When moving, the animal should display steps that are not heavy or plodding but give an impression of lightness and elasticity. Don't be put off by what may seem in the stable to be a somewhat lifeless creature, for even the best of animals will at times look like this, especially when resting after a meal. Horses and ponies are best observed out at pasture, where one can witness their movement and form in a completely natural state. If one observes a natural spring to the step as the animal trots up, and at faster paces a 'floating' over the ground, then one may safely assume verve to be present. (Always look at the horse's movement when the animal is on level ground. Even a slightly rising incline will exaggerate the normal action, as the forelegs will be carried slightly higher and the hocks engage more actively in order to provide the extra thrust and lift necessary to propel it forwards up the slope.)

The head

When evaluating a horse's conformation pay particular attention to the head, as it will indicate the character and disposition of the animal more than any other part. The eyes must be large and clear, reflecting kindness and confidence, and not be mean looking or sunken. They should be well set, wide apart and far enough down the forehead to allow good forward vision. When the horse looks at you it should do so with a steady gaze. If its eyes are continually moving and unsteady, what one might call a 'shifty' look, if they are rolled showing the whites, or if they are small and 'piggy', a troubled character and meanness is indicated. A vague, absent look is another bad sign as it suggests psychological disturbances and the horse will probably lack concentration when schooling is attempted. I am also suspicious of a pronounced 'hump' in the line of the forehead across the front between the eyes. This arching of the forehead is often a sign of unwillingness to accept discipline, and such horses and ponies are often very intractable. The ears, too, can indicate a lot: we want to see expressive ears that show alertness by their mobility; those that are fairly short and deeply arched indicate sensitivity.

If the head possesses eyes and ears of the type showing merit as described and the head is fairly lean and finely made, then spirit and verve of the type required will usually be present. However, not all breeds display the beauty of an Arab or Andalusian, and many European breeds of balance and achievement do have quite heavy heads, as may be seen among the warmbloods of Germany, Irish types and the Lipizzaner. But heads that do not possess most of the desired points should give rise to serious reservations about whether that particular horse or pony will be a satisfactory type to train and school on to anything but quite ordinary performance.

Upper foreleg

Provided that the thrust from the hindquarters is adequate, a well muscled front with a humerus bone of moderate length connected to the shoulder so as not to place it in too horizontal a plane will give a long-striding step. If, in addition to this, the elbow is 'free' so that it stands clear of the body and is not stuck to the side of the horse, the animal will be able to gallop freely and to get out of critical situations and remain on its four legs. Its trotting, too, will benefit from this freedom of the elbow. Forearms should be long compared to the cannon, and the knees large and flat to provide strong points of attachment for the ligaments and tendons.

Lower foreleg

The cannons should be broad and short, with well defined tendons that give an impression of leanness and strength. Pasterns should be sloping and elastic in action and the fetlocks flat-sided and 'clean', as puffiness in this region suggests lack of verve and staying power. If the angle of the pastern is too steep in an upright plane the inelastic thudding of the hoof will transmit unwanted concussion to the joints of the animal's legs, and through its frame to the rider also. This will result in premature wear to the animal's legs and early fatigue in the rider. At the other extreme an over-sloping pastern, especially when long, will make for a very comfortable ride but can often exert an excessive strain on the tendons, and this conformation therefore indicates potential weakness. Obviously much will depend on the inherent strength (or weakness) of the tendons and ligaments as to whether damage is likely to result. Strong tendons that support a sloping 'soft' pastern will result in a springy stride and one that allows the rider great contact with an undisturbed seat, especially at the sitting trot. A sloping pastern also allows for a compensating sliding action of the front hoofs when landing after jumping (not to be confused with slipping), which protects and assists the mechanism of the foot.

The feet

The shape and construction of the foot is a vital factor in any horse, as without good feet an otherwise faultless conformation and perfect disposition will be practically worthless. I like to see feet of reasonable size that are bell-shaped, have strongly formed walls and frogs together with a good deep heel and a vaulted sole.

Shallow heels and thin, flat soles lead to bruising and damage to the inner sensitive structures, particularly the pedal and navicular bones. If the horn is black and resilient then so much the better, although brittle and pale-coloured horn is not in itself a reason for rejecting an animal. As the foot is the part that supports all the weight of the animal and the rider, and is the first part to receive the concussion of impact with the ground when motion takes place, its importance can be appreciated. 'No foot – no horse' is an old and familiar saying; I make no excuse for repeating it here. Always look carefully at the shape and condition of a horse or pony's feet before buying, and after purchase care for them as a first priority. You will not regret it and much frustration and disappointment will be avoided. Never skimp on shoeing, and always be sure to discuss any problems with your farrier, and see to it that he has a sympathetic understanding of what is required and knows his business.

The back and chest

In seeking a riding horse that will comfortably perform its gaits with verve the back becomes very important, as the rider must be carried here while the whole mechanism of the horse or pony still works freely. Although we do not want a stiff, straight back nor do we want one that is unmistakably a sway back. Although the latter can be very comfortable they make extension difficult, to the detriment of correct dressage as well as of speed. A reasonable length of back is desirable as the horse will stand over more ground; if it is composed of a combination of long withers, long breastbone providing a level girth furrow, and not excessively long loins, it will be an ideal back. Such a shape will also indicate an animal that will 'do' well and be constitutionally sound. It will also be agile and find its balance more easily than a short-backed, 'square' horse, which will find it difficult to keep its balance because of the shortness of its area of support. On the other hand, an animal that is too large will also suffer when it comes to agility and balance.

Width and depth of the chest is also important as narrow-chested, long-legged horses will tire more rapidly because they lack room for heart and lung action. Being narrow and long-legged also means that they tend to become 'cross-legged' in their lateral movements, stepping too far out to the side and passing the line through the centre of gravity, thus losing their impulsion. Excessively long legs also tend to drag somewhat in the collected gaits. If the chest is over-round and wide, on the other hand, out of proportion to the body, the horse will be stuffy and lack manoeuvrability, and the rider will be unable to establish a good leg position in order to transmit his controls.

Hindquarters

In this region length is desirable, especially between the hips and the point of the buttocks, from the hips to the stifle and from the stifle to the point of the hock. This should be coupled with short cannons, thus placing the hocks as close as possible to the ground. The hock joint itself must be strongly built, with length and width and also depth – the distance between its inner and outer surfaces. This will enable the joint to carry and distribute the load of the horse's weight and that of the rider and to throw it forward under pressure by use of its lever action. It should be supported in this by good musculature of the second thigh, and a lower leg judged on the same principles as those determining the forelegs. Hind pasterns will, however, be less sloping than those at the front in normal conformation, as this is compensated for in the hind legs by the shock-absorbing action of the hocks. The perfectly shaped hock (if such a thing exists) is very hard to find or even to define, as so many factors will necessarily play a part in determining what is theoretically perfect. 'Open' hocks that place the lower leg further to the rear, or over-bent hocks that cause the horse to 'stand under' both have their critics, but I refrain from being dogmatic about it as many other compensating factors in a horse's conformation will determine if the resulting action is good or bad. What must be assessed in each case is whether the horse's overall shape enables it to use its hocks with complete freedom of action to produce a springy step in flexion and extension when completely collected.

Bowed hocks and those whose points are carried too close together when viewed from the rear can, because of the unfavourable angle when under load, lead to disease. When having to execute a turn while under load, bowed hocks will also tend to evade the correct bend and thus escape from the rider's control. They can also cause lack of impulsion and carrying ability. Cow hocks, where the points are angled together, can actually assist in negotiating difficult terrain, especially when travelling uphill. One such horse I owned would positively march uphill with terrific gusto at the walk in a way that no other horse I have ridden could match. I have witnessed other horses with this conformation and also those with sickle hocks (the two not infrequently go together) that were able to stand back on their hocks and accelerate away at great speed. What one must do is to observe and ride the animal to form an individual judgement about whether any particular 'suspect' point will act to the animal's disadvantage in training and schooling. This is where theory ends and practical use proves or disproves one's suspicions. What can be said is that horses or ponies displaying a tighter and denser texture to their tendons and musculature and having the sinewy appearance of the more highly bred type are less likely to have their efficiency affected by minor faults in conformation.

Musculature and framework

A horse or pony should, even when not in riding condition, display contours of musculature that show a predisposition to proper development. Its frame, too, should be such that one can see a good outline will result when the covering muscles have been developed. Viewed from the rear the hips should be level, as one-sidedness indicates disease of the leg. Wide hips indicate power, though as long as the distance between the stifle joints (laterally through the body) is greater than that between the two seat bones (ischium) animals with otherwise narrower hips can still produce a lot of power. Under the tail the thigh muscles should meet on their inner surface where they cover the femur, and not reveal a hollow gap. The tail itself is helpful in determining if the animal has verve – it should energetically resist being lifted. The dock should represent a continuation of the sacrum following the direction of the croup; if it hangs down at an abrupt angle between the hindquarters a lack of endurance and low-grade performance is indicated. The development resulting from proper training can improve a poorly attached tail, but little improvement should be expected in producing an acceptable tail carriage if it is naturally of the dangling type. I like to see the tail held clear from the buttocks when the horse is in motion, for without it the necessary enthusiasm, spirit and vigour – in one word, verve – will surely be missing.

During training the rider's skill will call upon the horse or pony to use its muscles with increased activity, and by gradually increasing his demands the trainer will bring about the development of the weaker parts and so strengthen the animal. With this gained strength it can then be asked to release the energy concealed within it and place the harmonious power of all its muscles at the willing service of its rider. But without a 'giving' character backed up by a good constitution, even after years of work any outstanding achievement will be doubtful. Only to a certain extent can the necessary qualities be seen in the exterior of a horse; much will depend on those that come from within. To save disappointment later, this should always be borne in mind when a horse is being purchased.

Not everyone can own a horse or pony of impeccable breeding or high potential – indeed the two do not necessarily go together. Not every horse or any favoured breed is a top-class performer, and as I have previously stated many less good-looking animals will outperform their better looking brothers. Nevertheless, it is a fundamental fact of human nature that we all like a thing not only to do good but also to look good, so the search for the ideal is ever present with horses as with everything. That is not to say that those already owning a horse or pony of somewhat doubtful ancestry or one that is rather ordinary in bearing should not bother to train it properly. Although only frustration and disappointment awaits those who try to reach the top with a second-class animal, by no means everyone wishes to reach the pinnacle of equestrian achievement. Many may not even be interested in any level of competition but merely wish to school their mounts to become more satisfactory and reliable rides for the sheer pleasure of it. These people will be just as delighted when their horse or pony responds to their moderate training as those able to coax *haute école* from their more highly trained mounts. Many older riders, especially, may only want to progress to a medium standard, having lost the first flush of youth and the desire to beat the world. For these people there is surely no better way to enjoy riding than on a horse that has been schooled by them to perform obediently those movements that give them pleasure.

3 Principles of riding and training

The supreme quality required to train any horse or pony is patience. The animal must also be treated with affectionate, but not sloppy, handling that rewards it with a pat or kind word when it complies with a demand. Punishment should only be given when strictly necessary, and not when clumsiness or inadequate understanding of what was required have caused a mistake. If the animal has psychological or physical shortcomings even greater patience will be needed if it is eventually to understand and respond correctly to the rider's controls. This is not to say that semi-compliance is acceptable, as precision during any form of gymnastic training must be insisted upon. But when the horse or pony has given the rider initial compliance during training it should never then be asked to go on until it becomes angrily excited or confused. Always cease immediately a new lesson has been learned and do not be tempted to go on enjoying the victory. Make sure the horse or pony is quiet and relaxed before returning to the stable; it will need time to calm down, and should never return with its nerves overstimulated by too long a session or by rough treatment during training. In this way the animal will be calm and ready to learn next time it is taken out, having absorbed the previous lesson in a calm and relaxed manner.

By this practice the rider and trainer will build up an understanding with his horse, which will guide the training programme and help to establish the natural limits to what the horse can do. The confidence between man and animal so essential in training will develop. This confidence is very hard to re-establish once it has been lost through brutality to the animal, and because of the horse's tremendous memory for things unpleasant a scar will persist that will surely lead to trouble. Do not confuse this advice by thinking that the rider and trainer need not be strong willed – on the contrary, no horse will respect weakness. It is always better to get compliance by diplomatic persuasion, but never avoid a struggle if the animal seeks to exploit you when you are yielding.

Never put yourself in a position where the animal's strength could get the better of what must at all times be your superior will and spirit. From this it will be understood why really expert riders and trainers are born rather than made; the delicate balance between strictness, kindness, dominant influence and reward that must be maintained only comes in a high degree to those born with a natural gift for it.

Influence of the seat

A well designed saddle will allow the rider's buttocks to rest in the middle of its lowest point and thus be nearest to the horse's back, and in this position the rider's weight should be supported by the lower edges of his two seat bones. The buttock muscles should be relaxed, allowing the pelvis to sink as low as possible to the surface of the saddle; if they are tensed or contracted they are forced up under the pelvis between the seat and the saddle. In the correct position the hips are vertical, and the width of the buttocks resting in the saddle allows the flattened inner surface of the thigh to be in contact with the side of the saddle and thus embrace the side of the horse. With stirrups adjusted for this position and a low, firm knee support, balance will be facilitated, as will the ability to respond truly to the motion of the horse. This is a normal seat. This position gives the flexibility necessary to compensate for rapid shifts of gravity, both forwards and sideways, and also protects the rider from fatigue as his centre of gravity is maintained without effort, enabling him to 'go along' with the horse. With the rider's upper body kept naturally upright above the vertical hips, and with the muscles of the small of the back relaxed and not cramped in tension, the rider will then follow and sustain the horse's movement and swing in harmony with it. This will absorb any shock waves produced by the horse's gait that are not ironed out by the knees and ankles, and so provide a deep seat that 'sticks' to the saddle. By means of a supple spine the rider will be said to have a 'soft' seat, which will allow him to sit out all the movements of his horse. Horses and ponies with slightly hollow backs and those with sloping pasterns will, by virtue of their smoother, less jarring movements, make this easier for the rider. Younger riders, too, will have an advantage over older ones, whose cartilage separations of joints and vertebrae have become somewhat hardened and less resilient with age.

The best exercise for learning the technique of the 'soft' seat is to ride a rather bouncy horse at the trot without stirrups and to 'tune' yourself to the oscillations from the saddle. Do not try to do this either by swinging your legs or by forcibly pulling yourself into the saddle by tightening your legs around the horse; nor should the back become sloppy and weak. Rather you must maintain balance

25

Influence of the seat: a normal seat. The rider's pelvis is low in the saddle, the hips vertical and the flattened inner surface of the thigh in contact with the saddle supported by a firm knee.

and contact by rhythmically allowing your muscles to respond in harmony with the movement and rhythm of the horse.

Head and shoulders

The rider's head plays a more important part in maintaining balance and a correct seat than is generally realized. It should be held high, with square but relaxed shoulders, as stiffness in this area will inevitably be transmitted to the rest of the body. The general appearance should be one of calm self-confidence. Never slouch in the saddle or allow the head to wobble loosely about, as this will prevent the correct use of the back and seat controls. A rider's head weighs a considerable amount, and placed as it is at the end of his frame has a considerable effect on his centre of gravity and his balance. Imagine a brick attached to the end of a long cane held in an upright position, and you will appreciate the importance of not allowing your head to hang down or wobble

26

about, which will produce a false distribution of weight. Any unwanted movement or badly distributed weight in the rider will reflect down to the horse and bring about an unwanted response. Remember that the animal is being trained to listen to your controls and respond to them, and any undesirable weight changes or false messages that you transmit will only serve to confuse it. Always keep your chin in, as this will naturally lift the chest and not cause a hollowing of the back, which is a very bad fault in riders who have not achieved suppleness. The Spanish rider has much to teach us when it comes to looking stylish in the saddle. He sits very erect but without any trace of awkwardness or stiffness, and looks very proud, in complete character with his horse. He holds the reins in one hand, with the other placed jauntily on his thigh, and from this position nearly all directions and impulsion controls flow from seat and legs to his mount. Another example of correct riding position is that of the riders of the Spanish Riding School of Vienna. These men maintain their upper body in perfect equilibrium, and indeed it is said that their horses become so finely tuned to changes in the rider's balance and weight distribution that they can be made to canter to the left or right merely by the movement of the rider's head to that side! During my visits to the Vienna school I cannot say that I bore witness to this claim, but it does show the importance that is given to the upper part of the rider's body in relation to the horse's training.

Influence of the hands

I dealt with the relative position of the hands in Chapter 1, so here I shall consider their specific use. There are trainers who insist that the rider should always maintain the position of the hands at a set distance apart and held just above the pommel. But when this takes no account of the position of the horse's head, the instruction is wrong. The position of the hands must always be considered in conjunction with the degree of collection of the horse, and will also vary when teaching a young horse in order to encourage a certain head position. It will also vary with the use of different types of bit. Do not conclude from this that the hands alone can be used to shape the outline of the horse, as this is not so. No amount of hand variation will have the desired effect unless backed up by strong seat and leg controls. The hands should have a positive contact with the bit, but there should be an elastic response when the horse seeks to stretch for the bit as a result of the driving controls. The more this can be felt, the more supple and responsive the horse is. The rider can then influence the horse's poise, pace and direction by a whole range of controls, from the slightest opening or closing of the fingers to a complete turning in of the hands or withdrawal of the upper arms. Even when more energetic hand controls are used they should still be elastic in their movement and never hard and unyielding. Start off by 'asking' with the slightest squeeze of the fingers, and when you need to be more energetic never allow the movement to become an unfeeling pull on the horse's mouth. Always be ready to give at the slightest sign of compliance from the horse or you will produce resistance from the animal and eventually a hard mouth will result which will do only harm.

In horses and ponies advanced in their training the slight displacement of the reins by a sideways movement of the hands will bring about a desired change in direction. With a young horse, moving one hand to the side with the palm turned upwards will make it easier for the animal to begin its turn and also to maintain its balance if supported by the opposite rein. While on the subject of rein control I will mention here my preference for the type of rein used. Although many people profess the advantages of narrow reins of plain leather, I prefer the plaited or laced leather type for two reasons: first, because plain leather becomes much too slippery with a sweating horse or when riding in the rain; second, I find that the 'notches' allow me greater feel as I can exert pressure without the leather creeping through my fingers. I also prefer this type of rein on the snaffle bit when using a double bridle, though I use a plain rein on the curb bit so as not to have too much bulk to hold. Soft leather gloves can also help provide a better, more sensitive grip, but preferences such as this can be worked out by the individual to suit his or her requirements. I do believe, though, that rubber-covered reins are too bulky, though they give a good grip, and 'feel' is lost for training purposes; plaited nylon reins are harsh on the fingers.

Riding with both hands is standard practice when training the young horse. This allows the outer hand to be advanced in turns, while the lateral 'opening' of the inner rein helps the inexperienced horse or pony to understand this control. Two hands also give the rider broader control in conjunction with the use of the lower body. When jumping it is also essential to have both hands in control of the reins in order to yield fully on both sides of the animal's neck. However, there are occasions when riding with one hand can be helpful. A rider who has not yet achieved a fully compliant and flexible seat can communicate some of his stiffness to the horse by holding the reins too rigid, which will also disturb his seat. In this case, having him ride with the reins held in one hand will have the effect of tiring his convulsive hold more quickly so he will 'release' the horse more. The horse will then respond by releasing its cramped muscles and relaxing its back, which in turn allows the rider to sit better and more softly. Riding with one hand may also be advisable when teaching a young horse its first steps in *piaffe* if the rider tends to 'saw' at his horse's mouth by overdoing the alternating left–right, left–right rein controls often advocated for this movement. As soon as the reins are transferred to one hand the horse will respond to the gentler guidance, stretch to reach the bit and relax its back. When this happens it will learn the transition to the *piaffe* with much less difficulty. There is nothing mysterious in this – riding with one hand automatically encourages the rider to relax in an upright sitting position and to ride with a soft seat. I also believe it to be easier when stronger use of the small of the back is required to support restraining control from the legs with the upper body leaning back. When riding with one hand the free arm should hang straight down naturally from the shoulder, with the hand held just behind the thigh and the palm turned inwards towards the horse. With riders who have not yet acquired an independent soft seat any other position will tend to produce unconscious stiffness in the rider.

Many horses that are pullers will move more calmly when the rider ceases to try restraint with both hands and reverts to holding the reins in one hand, and many others will trot and canter more freely when ridden single-handed and thus be prevented from tightening up. Once again I will refer to the Spanish rider and also to the Western style of riding. Their mounts, ridden with one hand, show extreme suppleness and manoeuvrability, especially when swinging or pushing off from the hocks. It goes back to what I said earlier – the secret of the hands lies in the possession of a good deep seat, and this can be more easily achieved when riding with one hand. It is no good, for example, hanging on to a bolting horse with both hands and allowing it to pull you forwards out of a loose seat with the resulting loss of the restraining leg controls. The rider's weight must be fixed by the pelvis pressing firmly into the saddle so that any divisive action or bucking from the horse can be counteracted by the small of the back and the buttocks. This is why strong men can sometimes be carried off by a horse that presents no such problems to a physically weaker rider. The weaker man has learned to use the small of his back to 'fix' his seat. The same principle is applied when a tug-of-war is won by a weaker opponent who has anchored his weight better.

Types of seat

I have left until now the explanation of variations in the types of seat as I did not want to confuse the issue, knowing only too well how too much jargon and theoretical text can 'explode' the reader's mind.

The first variation of the normal seat is the forward or jumping seat, sometimes also referred to as the crotch seat. This is used for a specific purpose in jumping or cross-country riding, and should not be confused with what is often mistakenly called a crotch seat that is produced by riding with stirrups that are too long or on

Types of seat: a forward or jumping seat, demonstrated by the author using one hand thus proving correct balance, with a firm knee position supporting the weight of his forward inclination.

badly designed saddles. In these latter instances the rider is placed onto the forward edges of his seat bones without the counteracting support of the knee. Having to reach for overlong stirrups is bad as it loosens the seat and upsets balance. The proper forward seat is produced by the rider taking his weight further forwards to relieve pressure on the horse's back and hindquarters, and it cannot be maintained in this position without the active support of the knee. The rider's back is inclined forwards as he goes with the movement of the horse, and his weight is carried on the forward edges of the pelvic seat bones and on the thighs. The knee, in contact with the saddle on either side, supports this forward inclination of the rider's balance and allows the rider to help the horse negotiate a jump or extend at a full gallop. Shorter stirrups are used with this seat, and also a saddle shaped with a forward-cut panel to allow the more forward position of the knee. In the forward seat the rider's knees and heels will be forced downwards and he will be able to 'ride out' bumps and irregularities over rough terrain, rising in the saddle from the knee, which is 'fixed', and allowing the knees and ankles to absorb the shocks. The stirrups must also be shortened because when extended at the gallop a horse's body lengthens and thus becomes thinner; if the rider is not to be

30

bounced out of the stirrups he must have them shorter to allow for their relatively lower displacement as the animal stretches out. An extreme example of shortened stirrups can be seen in the very short knee position used by jockeys in racing, where it is necessary for them to have a forward anchor point (the knee) to push against and thus prevent the galloping horse from pulling them too far forwards up its neck. This latter position is not one that need bother the ordinary rider as it is unsuitable for normal purposes, and in any case it provides little or no lateral support for the rider – as shown by the easy 'unshipping' of the jockey when a racehorse swings sideways.

The other type of seat derived from the basic normal seat is used to produce more drive from the saddle. The rider's pelvis is pushed forwards by contracting the small of the back, and his weight is pressed downwards so that his hips slope backwards and the rear edges of the seat bones carry more of his weight. This has the effect of pushing the horse forwards with greater impetus.

The driving seat: the rider's pelvis is pushed forwards and downwards, thus creating greater thrust from the horse's hocks and causing the centre of gravity to shift further to the rear.

31

The leg

The rider's legs implement the controls that produce forward movement in the horse and maintain that movement once it has begun. Only after this has happened can the rider use his weight to drive the animal on. Pressure from the leg should cease as soon as obedience has been achieved or the horse will grow impervious to it. Repeated tapping of the legs will prevent continuous contact and 'feel' between the rider's legs and the horse. When not being used to apply direct control, the legs of the rider must remain in light contact with the horse and move only gently in rhythm to the horse's movement. Never develop the bad habit of letting your legs swing to and fro or that of their continually hitting against the horse.

The rider's leg, located just behind the girth, always exerts the stimulating pressure that produces forward impetus; when it lies somewhat further behind the girth it exerts control to prevent the quarters swinging out and the horse from leaving the track; alternatively, it asks the horse to do just that, depending on the rider's other controls. In the first instance the rider's leg behind the girth is acting as a restraining influence, and in the second it is producing lateral drive. When leg controls are applied they are supported by an increased forward thrust of the seat and the small of the back, with a corresponding increase in the pushing down of the knee and heel. When the rider exerts equal pressure of both legs the horse begins to move forwards; when it is already moving this equal pressure will accelerate the gait. It is the driving force. Later a horse will learn that this pressure may also mean increased collection. It will also learn to move away from the lateral driving controls of the rider's leg exerted farther back behind the girth.

If the horse does not pay enough attention to the rider's leg controls they can be intensified by the use of a stick or schooling whip. This must be of sufficient length to reach behind the rider's leg to reinforce the controls being given without the rider having to change the position of his arm and hand. It can also be used to make a sulky horse pay attention or a lazy one wake up. Spurs can also be used for this, and although I know of many horsemen (especially those in Spain) who punish disobedience with spurring, I think that their best use is as a refinement of the leg controls at later stages of training. However, when used by a long-legged rider or one whose stirrup length places his heel well below the horse's body they can be quite ineffective unless swan-necked spurs are used and buckled high up the boot. I have watched with amusement many riders who work away without their spurs ever coming near the horse's side!

In the normal riding position on a conventional English saddle the rider's heels should be slightly lower than the toes, as it is in this position that he can most effectively use the muscles of his legs, which must contract and relax elastically. The stirrups should be of a length that allows the inside of the thigh to be closed on the saddle, with the ball of the foot positioned on the stirrup bar underneath the body – that is to say, not pushed forwards. Stirrup lengths will vary depending on individual riders, the horse's shape and the shape of the saddle. This is why in saddles designed for dressage, when the rider's leg must be carried lower with longer stirrups, the saddle panel is straighter and more upright. On the other hand, a jumping saddle is made with a rounder, forward-reaching panel to accommodate shorter stirrups and the higher and more forward knee position necessary for a jumping seat. The shape of general-purpose or all-purpose saddles is somewhere in between, depending on the maker's particular design. For most people a well made saddle of this kind will be quite satisfactory for their needs, both for jumping and for dressage, as long as they remember that it will limit the length of their stirrups. I have seen instructors who insist on making their pupils ride too long in the wrong type of saddle and then wonder why they are unable to maintain their balance or acquire a good seat. Provided that the saddle fits the rider and the horse, when the correct length of stirrup has been found for normal use (including dressage) it will be possible to shorten the stirrups by two to four holes for jumping. It can in fact be quite an advantage always to use the same saddle when training a young horse, as the animal will more easily become familiar with the controls and weight distribution of the rider. When choosing the correct saddle and the best length of stirrup I believe it is better to err on the side of one hole too short rather than one hole too long, especially for older riders. If they are a bit short the rider's legs will not have quite the same grip but the seat will be firmer, providing steadier control. When the stirrups are too long the rider will be tilted forwards and his seat loosened. I know it is fashionable to ride long, but when overdone it unbalances both horse and rider. A spell of riding without stirrups will improve and deepen the rider's seat if it is felt that extra stirrup length is desirable.

Another mistake some instructors make is to require their pupils to hold their feet parallel to the sides of the horse. This is wrong because contact is lost between the lower leg below the knee and the animal's flanks; if this contact is not to be lost the rider must then turn his foot under the horse from the ankle. This too is wrong, as it stiffens the joint and the whole leg loses its springiness. Again, proper control is lost. The other extreme of turning the toes outwards at an acute angle positions the whole of the lower leg wrongly and places the rider's calf on the horse in such a way as to squeeze the animal incorrectly. The rider's foot should always lie at a natural angle, with the toe turned slightly away from the horse. This natural position, with the toe forcibly turned neither outwards nor inwards, will result in the inner edge of the stirrup assuming a position slightly lower than the outer edge, as may be seen when observing the rider's feet from a position in front of the horse. The foot should rest on the stirrup bar at an angle from the little toe to the bunion joint of the big toe. The build of the rider as well as that of the horse affects the position of the rider's legs; instructors would do well to remember that we cannot successfully press all riders into one set positon or kind of seat.

To conclude this chapter I should like to make it clear that except when teaching a very young horse or pony to understand the meaning of each control, when it may be necessary to apply with separate emphasis a particular control, all the controls should work together and be applied in coordination with each other. The rider must be able to produce a balanced response from the whole horse, not from just part of it. The rider's seat, legs, weight and hands must act in unison, and the variation in intensity of each part will depend on what instruction is being given.

4 Early training of the young horse or pony

For the purpose of this book I shall assume that your young horse or pony has come to you already backed and lightly ridden, and that you are now ready to begin its training. (The next book in this series, *Small-scale Breeding*, will deal with the handling, bitting and breaking of young stock.) Serious training should not begin until the horse is between four and five years old in the riding horse, as it could cause damage that would affect the horse's soundness in later life.

One of the best methods of strengthening and settling a young horse or pony (or any new acquisition) is to ride it out in open country. For the first few weeks this exercise should be restricted to short periods and be done at the walk. Let the animal get used to you and the local environment, and try to calm it and gain its confidence while it is being exercised. Never punish it at this stage for misbehaviour when strange objects or unfamiliar sights are encountered, but instead persevere with persuasion until you have gained the horse's obedience and confidence. It is very important that you always succeed in the end, however long it may take. The animal will come to respect you and to realize that nothing terrible will happen to it when you ask it to do something. Some young horses will take fright at or regard with the utmost suspicion the most insignificant objects – even a discarded cigarette packet can sometimes be enough – and yet take not the slightest notice of thundering juggernauts or noisy motor cycles. Many horses do not like things that lurk, such as walkers who stand back in hedgerows as you approach. All of these things, and they are numerous, will serve to unsettle or spook the young horse, and only by your calm and determined persuasion will its fears be overcome.

Adjusting to the rider's weight

At this early stage the animal's bones, ligaments and tendons are 'green', and the horse or pony will need to adjust to the addition of

35

the rider's weight and find its balance as well as gaining the necessary strength. If you are patient this will gradually happen. The animal will benefit from considerate handling in many ways, not least a longer useful life with less likelihood of unsoundness. Also make sure at the beginning that your saddle and the rest of your tack fit perfectly, as you do not want to inflict a sore back or cause misbehaviour such as bucking on account of ill-fitting or uncomfortable tack.

As the weeks go by, start to trot the horse or pony and include hilly country in its work to build up its muscles, especially those of the quarters. Do not work it at more than a walk when going downhill, however, as this places a strain on the forelegs and it will not be ready for this with the additional weight of a rider.

With many owners this working in open country will have to suffice for the preparation and future training of their horse or pony for the job it has to do. Provided that the animal is of the right type and responds freely, and the rider sufficiently qualified to enable him or her to train the animal in these circumstances, a fair amount can be accomplished. However, training of a gymnastic nature in the controlled environment of a manège or riding hall will have undeniable advantages for both horse and rider, for it is here that good horsemanship and proper schooling will enable the animal more readily to improve its balance, gait and poise. Sensible training in a schooling arena will supple the horse and teach it to relieve the burden carried by its legs through proper use of a supple and elastic back; this in turn will cause less fatigue to horse and rider; its legs will then cover more ground and with more spring to its steps the animal's joints will not be worn out prematurely. A combination of open country work and schooling in the confines of an arena provides the ideal method of training.

Improving thrust and impulsion

To improve the thrust that gives an increased forward impulsion, the horse must use its hind legs and engage them further forward towards the combined centre of gravity of itself and of the rider. It will not do so naturally; it needs the rider's influence in the application of dressage training. This can only be achieved once the muscles on either side of the spine have been strengthened sufficiently to allow the back to pulsate in a straight line, carrying the weight equally and evenly along a single track. If the back muscles are held rigidly they will act in tension rather than elastic pulsation, causing a sluggish dragging of the hind legs, which remain grounded for too long. When deciding upon the desired extent of forward reach required of the hind legs it must be remembered that only at the free gaits (when the combined centre of gravity of horse and rider is further forward) will the hind feet track up in front of the trace made by the forefeet. At the collected gaits this combined centre of gravity shifts further to the rear and the hind legs, bearing more of the load, will necessarily alight behind the trace of the front hoofs. In these collected positions, however, the hind leg must be bent to carry the load with an active pushoff and vigorous thrust brought about by the correct pulsating of the back.

For the moment our young horse or pony will only have strengthened to the extent that it can carry its own weight and that of its rider with balance at the free gaits, so we must work first of all at the free walk to encourage the hind legs to act further forwards and not to drag behind. This will make the back stretch out and flex itself, thus pulsating more powerfully, which will cause a stretching of the entire spinal column through to the neck enabling the horse to reach forwards for the bit. The rider brings

Teaching the young horse to stretch forwards for the bit at the free walk. The rider's driving leg controls are maintained, while the reins are gradually shortened as the horse finds and accepts the bit.

37

this about by use of the driving controls of his legs, which should cease to drive the horse as soon as it complies. At the same time the rider's hands must at first yield, so that in stretching forwards the horse can find its own balance and not use the reins for support. When it is moving forwards freely, with longer, rhythmic strides, the rider asks for more forward stretching by using the leg controls, and as this is given he holds his hands steady, accepting the pull from the horse's mouth but yielding elastically to the forward pulsations flowing through the animal's body to its mouth. In this way the animal will come to trust the bit and not be put off by sudden jolting that causes it pain. Later, this passive action of the hands sympathetically following the rhythm of the horse will bring about a supple coordination of the muscles of the poll and the masseter muscles (those of the jaw) thus allowing the animal's head to 'soften'. This coordination will in turn produce a responsive 'chewing' of the bit, producing saliva. This can only be properly achieved if the rider's seat is supple and independent: the rider will then begin to 'tune in' to his mount, to feel the pulsating muscles of the horse's back and the forward reach of the hindquarters as they carry more of the load and thereby lift the forehand. The horse's ribs will flatten and provide a firmer position for the supple 'breathing' of the rider's legs against the horse's sides. The rider now has more of the horse in front of him, so to speak, with the neck extended but rising up to the poll, and he can feel the horse filling the space between his legs and providing the proper position for the normal seat without stiffness. When this condition is satisfied, the driving controls of the rider's legs will have brought about the beginning of the horse's transition from natural balance to that of equestrian poise.

Coordinating leg and seat controls

When suppleness has been combined with forward thrust and impulsion by the use of the rider's leg controls, the next step is to combine this forward-driving action of the legs with that of the seat. The horse is now ready to absorb the combined instruction and react to it positively. The rider simply pushes his pelvis forwards by bracing the small of his back; the resulting pressure of his seat bones from back to front will transmit a forward thrust to the horse. The rider's upper body will automatically be lifted, and with the bracing of the back the hand will receive support to sustain the combined driving action of seat and legs. The combined use of the rider's seat and legs also shifts his weight slightly to the rear, with the result that the horse's hindquarters, which are already engaged under its body because of the rider's driving leg controls, are called upon to bend even more to cope with the additional load. Once the rider feels that this increased burden has

Driving force is produced by the rider exerting equal pressure with his legs; knee and heel are pushed downwards, supported by increased forward thrust of the seat by bracing the small of the back.

The working trot: combined impulsion and thrust produced by the rider's leg and seat controls is seen in the elastic, springy movement of the animal's legs. Spur and stick are ready to act as a sharp reminder to lazy or withholding animals.

39

been accepted and taken up by the hindquarters he must immediately return to his normal seat, and once again go along in rhythm with the horse's movement. If he does not, the horse will try to escape from this uninterrupted pressure by ceasing to engage its hindquarters, letting them fall behind. This will then place more load on the forelegs and cause the animal's back to hollow, disturbing the harmony of the gait. In equestrian terms the horse is then said to have fallen upon its shoulders. This seat control is essentially the same when used to accelerate the horse or to reduce or interrupt the pace. The difference is determined by the corresponding use of the rein control.

Working at the trot

The rider's ability to make the hindquarters bend more vigorously and provide additional thrust is his means of converting the ordinary natural trot into a working trot. The horse will lift its neck, extending it both forwards and upwards, with a corresponding shortening of the reins. When driving the horse forwards at the working trot the rider must not apply constant leg driving controls and force the horse to ever hastier running. He must only apply them to produce a rate of trot somewhat faster than the horse's natural speed. This will vary with the type and conformation of the individual horse and differences in lengths of stride. What we should observe is the combined impulsion and thrust produced by the rider's leg controls in an elastic, springy movement of the animal's legs both on leaving the ground and when alighting. This working trot will form the basis for future training because it ensures active involvement of the muscles and joints without overburdening them. Also, as the animal has only two legs grounded simultaneously and they are there for a shorter time than when walking, it is more difficult for the animal to evade the rider's influence. The increased impulsion makes it more difficult for the horse to hold back in an arbitrary manner.

Short periods of canter may be allowed at this stage of training as it will help to promote impulsion, and the horse will be ready for this as soon as it willingly begins to canter when being ridden in open country. But serious schooling at the canter will not come until later in its training, as the young horse's joints could suffer from the increased loads thrust upon them at this gait in the confines of the schooling arena. At this stage the young horse will not be sufficiently advanced to carry itself correctly at the canter. (Note: the word canter is the English term for the pace of three-time. On the Continent there is no equivalent term, and the word gallop is used for this as well as the faster gait.) If the schooling arena is large enough to allow corners to be taken in a gentle curve, and the young horse is able to carry itself in balance to a fair degree at this pace, working at the canter for short periods will aid suppleness. The working trot, though, will be the primary gait and it must be a combination of regular, well-timed, lively and lengthy strides. The horse must go forwards briskly, swinging its hind legs and using its back in elastic cooperation so as to relieve the loads on its legs. The rider must encourage this vigorous movement without promoting stiffness or tightness, or hurrying or holding back.

The change from a natural trot to a working trot at the beginning of a lesson is achieved by a gradual increasing of the controls to produce a lengthened and more powerful stride from the hind legs while the speed of the trot is maintained. Merely increasing the speed is valueless if this timing is lost. If the gait becomes hurried the irregular, smooth resistance by the hands in shortening the reins with the legs remaining passive, will serve to moderate the gait. The amount of rein control will depend on the horse's reaction to being asked for increased work. Some may display high spirits and leap about or become frightened when asked to work harder, and in these cases a long rein will give too much freedom and result in the reins being snatched up, losing their steadiness, whenever an emergency arises. If the reins are held comparatively short and low, remaining in contact with the horse's mouth whatever the situation, the animal will be brought to order more quickly and return to calmer movement. As it becomes less tense, the horse will regain its timing and seek to stretch forwards once again to meet the rider's hands as they now advance and lengthen the rein. With suppleness regained as all tension evaporates, the rider's hands can return to their position in front of his body and the young horse will surrender itself to its rider, having learned not to tighten up or become excited during exercise.

In dealing with young animals that are lazy and withholding, a sharp reminder with the stick or a touch of the spurs will serve to focus their attention to duty and make them advance more readily. Cease the punishment as soon as a response is forthcoming and praise the animal, letting it go forwards a few strides on a 'free' rein. Do make sure, though, that your preparatory work has been sufficiently gradual and progressive to ensure that weakness is not mistaken for unwillingness, as punishment should never be meted out to a weak horse that has insufficient muscular strength to respond correctly to the demands made upon it.

Transitions: trot to walk, walk to halt and vice versa

Now that the horse has become supple and learned responsive compliance to the rider's controls it can be brought to a walk from the trot and then halted not by merely coming to a stop. The rider's seat will remain in the saddle and not follow the movement so freely, as the hands ask the horse to slow down for a transition to the walk. When this is achieved the rider's weight will then be displaced towards the quarters by the pressure of his seat, and the resisting action of his hands will cause an immediate halt. The rider's legs are kept in readiness to ask for forward movement again and to resist any attempt to step backwards. During this early training we must allow the animal to stretch its neck forwards and down to rest and stretch its muscles. When the horse walks on

When a slight relaxing of the rein after halting causes the horse to play with the bit and produce saliva while standing still, it is an invaluable sign that the animal trusts and accepts the bit.

again the reins must first be taken up and the horse allowed to move forwards in a free, unhurried walk with reins of a good length, the gait long-striding and relaxed. When changing up to the trot, gradually shorten the reins so that the walk sequence does not suffer and then start off the trot from this position. Proper schooling at the walk will come only after the horse or pony is able to carry itself properly with full responsiveness at the trot. Another important factor at this stage of training is to relax the reins (but not to surrender contact with the bit) after the horse has made the transition from the trot to walk or after a halt has been made, in order to encourage the horse to chew the bit. By gradually opening his fingers the rider encourages the horse or pony to stretch the muscles of its back and neck and play with the bit, thus producing saliva. This is an invaluable guide in reassuring us that the horse's training has been accomplished in such a way as to make it trust and accept the bit. It can then quickly be taught to stand still calmly with the reins completely loosened, and now is the time to pat it and use the voice to give praise and encouragement. This will help in its training, and your tone of voice will also play a significant part in getting the horse to understand when it has done well. I do not believe in the practice used by many of giving titbits as a reward during training, as trying to eat with the bit in position can cause the animal some difficulty and it may get its tongue over the bit.

If the horse seeks to free its head immediately the rider gives it the reins after a halt by throwing its head about and jerking it up and down, we should ask ourselves if our work has been faulty and has made the animal feel uncomfortable by being forcibly held together with rough controls. Another indication that all is not well is when the horse moves crookedly, one hind leg evading the requirements being asked of it. This must not be allowed to develop and become ingrained, and the rider must concentrate even more on preventing stiffness setting in by riding the horse fowards with even loading on both sides. Crookedness is likely to be present in most young horses to some degree: This is natural with all creatures, including humans, who are not fully trained gymnastically to perform equally well on both sides. This can be dealt with more successfully later, once the horse has learned lateral flexion and impulsion in response to the rider's controls. At this early stage our concern must be not to induce worse crookedness by trying to shape the young horse with excessive influence of the hands.

First stage collection

Once the young horse or pony has progressed to the stage where a positive contact with the bit can be obtained, we can now shorten the reins without interfering with the gait or free activity of the back. If, however, this more positive contact does induce tension in the hindquarters and back it will be felt unpleasantly in the rider's seat, and the stiffening of the animal's neck will produce too hard a contact with the bit. The horse may also hollow its back and point its nose in a stargazing attitude. This indicates that we are making excessive demands upon the hindquarters and back, which have not yet been made strong enough for this degree of collection. When this happens the horse must be ridden forwards to improve its carriage, or the increased weight on the hindquarters will only teach the young horse to stiffen its hind joints in an effort to cope. This will produce a false gait and carriage. If there are no such adverse reactions we can assume that our training is advancing satisfactorily.

5 Lungeing and long-reining

Lungeing a young horse that has already been brought into service under saddle is an excellent way of strengthening both the framework and the confidence of the animal at the beginning of its training. It is also invaluable in retraining animals that have faulty gaits or tensions as a result of earlier mishandling.

At the beginning of training on the lunge it is best to use nothing more than the lungeing cavesson with a lungeing rein and whip. Make sure that the cavesson is well fitting, that the cheekpieces do not come too close to the animal's eyes and the noseband does not come too low down but fits snugly around the bony part of the nose where it cannot restrict breathing. Buckle the noseband tight enough to ensure that it does not slip or pull round once the horse or pony is working on a circle. If it does this the animal will become unbalanced and the outside cheekstrap will press against the eye. Discomfort from ill-fitting equipment will prevent quiet, unhurried, supple exercise from being performed. When the cavesson is satisfactorily fitted, attach the lungeing rein and lead the horse to the training area to begin work. The area can be an outdoor or indoor school. For those without these facilities a corner of a paddock is quite adequate provided that it is level and not slippery. A proper 'all-weather' surface is undoubtedly a great advantage both for lungeing and for ridden training, and for those interested in building their own outdoor school I shall include a section on how this can be done.

The lungeing area must be large enough to allow work on a large circle that will not restrict the young animal, especially if it becomes excited and capers about, as this will put unwanted strain on its joints. The lungeing rein should also be long enough to allow for this freedom, and be about 25 ft (8 m) long. Whether the rein is made of nylon, webbing or rope will be a matter of personal preference. Nylon is stronger but can be abrasive to the user's hands, and webbing does tend to snap suddenly with age. With the actual cavesson I do urge that a really good leather one is

45

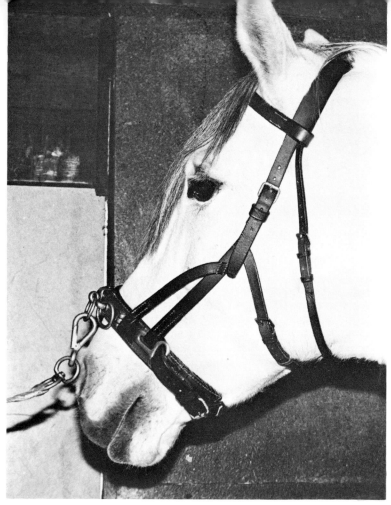

A well fitting leather cavesson: the cheek straps are well clear of the animal's eyes, and the noseband fits well up on the bony part of the nose where it cannot restrict breathing.

obtained, as these fit much better without the tendency to slip that the nylon types have. The buckles will be of better quality and are easier to fasten and undo. This can be crucial when handling inexperienced animals, which may fidget or play up; difficult buckles can easily cause an accident to the handler's fingers.

Voice commands

Work on the lunge begins by leading the horse around the perimeter of the schooling area to the left with the lunge rein clipped to the inside ring of the cavesson. Walk at the animal's inside shoulder, with the whip and loosely coiled spare length of rein in the left hand. Hold the rein leading to the cavesson in your right hand, allowing about a yard (metre) to be played out between you and the horse. This will allow the animal enough rein to stretch its neck and walk forwards naturally under no constraint. (We begin to the left because most horses and ponies go this way more easily.) If the horse tries to rush forward, shorten the rein and hold it back until it learns to walk forward quietly. If it holds back, use the whip by swinging it round behind you to tap the animal's hocks or quarters to gentle it forward. One's voice should be used to help make the animal learn what is required; the actual words of command do not matter as long as they come naturally to you and are repeated identically each time. Generally speaking slower, more drawn out commands will be spoken (or sung) to produce a slowing down of pace, and sharper, more abrupt words will be used to increase pace or gait. The exception to this in my own case is that I use a drawn-out 'a-n-d' followed by a crisp 'halt' to bring the animal to a stop.

Continue this walking round exercise until the animal stops on command and walks on again freely when asked, and also trots beside you from the walk and back again when you slow down and ask it to walk. Practise this in the other direction by clipping the lunge rein to the right side of the cavesson, first checking that nothing has slipped or become uncomfortable. Soon you will be able to let the horse walk on away from you while playing out the lunge rein and transferring the whip to your other hand so that it acts as a driving influence as the animal begins to describe a large circle around you. Get it to walk round in a large circle, changing pace and halting as before to voice command. When this stage is reached you should position yourself in the centre of the circle made by the horse and revolve on the spot. When evasions take place it may be necessary to shorten the lunge and move towards the horse or pony to help its understanding and encourage it to do what you require. Walk a small inner circle, endeavouring to keep the circumference of the animal's circle the same. After ironing out the problem return to your original position in the centre. Remember that you are lungeing the animal and not vice versa!

Once the animal is calmly circling you to the left, your left hand holding the lunge rein should be held steady with the rein taut enough to support the animal as it circles. The animal should go round with its shoulder level with you; hold the whip passively in your right hand, and use it to give a gentle swish aimed at the hocks to encourage the horse forwards if it slackens. When asking for a change of pace downwards, choose an opportune moment to give the command asking for a walk when the trot has slackened or for a halt when the animal is walking slowly; it is no good calling for a halt if the animal is going hurriedly forwards. In this way obedience to the voice will be learned by the horse or pony in a

Early work on the lunge: keep the rein steady, and taut enough to support the animal as it finds its balance; the whip should be used to encourage the animal forwards but not to frighten it; the trainer remains calm and relaxed at all times.

natural association with the transitions.

If, as often happens, the horse or pony gallivants around and generally explodes with high spirits, let it tire itself out while you remain calm. For the moment attempts to slow it down would prove fruitless and violent tugging on the lunge rein will hurt the animal and only worsen matters. If there is a danger of it slipping up or if the cavesson has become misplaced during these antics, the lesser evil of shortening the lunge rein to decrease the circle will become necessary until the animal has to reduce its pace and quieten down. This should be avoided if possible, as serious injury can be inflicted on young bones and joints that are forced to travel

A gentle canter on a large circle will do no harm, but beware of over-excited cavorting about; if this happens try to maintain a large circle to lessen the risk of injury to the animal's joints.

in a tight circle. If the circle is large enough then childish cavorting about will do no harm – it is in fact a natural reaction – but if it happens continually the chances are that you are overfeeding the animal for the work being done, and the remedy is obvious.

When things are going satisfactorily on a circle to the left you will need to work the horse in the opposite direction. At first you do this by bringing the horse quietly to a halt and walking out to it as it stands still. Walk towards its shoulder with your lowered whip in front of you to prevent the horse from coming in towards you, as crafty animals can learn to do this as a form of evasion. If it stays still reward it with a kind word and a pat when you reach it, buckle the lunge rein on the other side ring and turn the animal to face in the opposite direction. Encourage it to walk on away from you and retreat to your former central position and work on the other hand. If it tends to drift towards you from the circle, point your whip forwards to aim at its shoulder and so 'push' it out again. If this does not work and the horse persistently comes in and loosens the lunge rein, try raising the whip and swinging it downwards onto the lunge. At first this may also cause the horse to speed up but it will soon learn to step out on the circle. Later, all that need be done to get it to move out again is to 'rattle' the lunge rein gently.

When you ask for a halt it is also good practice to take a short step backwards, as many animals will learn that this movement accompanied by the voice command means they must stop. A gentle flexing of the wrist to produce a slight tug to the lunge rein will also encourage a decrease in pace from trot to walk if the voice command is not enough at first. Aways give praise by voice immediately a correct response has been obtained, and at the end of the lesson give the horse or pony a nice pat and reward it with its feed or a titbit as soon as it returns to the stable.

Of course all this is much easier, especially with stubborn or difficult horses, if you have an assistant to help you. The assistant's job will be to lead the horse or to walk behind it to encourage it forwards while you stay at the end of the lunge rein in the centre of the circle. This will be a great help in teaching the correct response to your voice commands and to bring forward the next stage in the lungeing programme.

Greater demands on the lunge

With this next stage you begin the lesson by clipping the lungeing rein onto the centre ring of the cavesson and then follow the same procedure as before except when you want to change direction. After working on a left circle with the rein in your left hand and the whip held in your right hand, bring the horse or pony to a halt. Now change the rein and whip to the other hand, take a step or two to the left and gently pull with your right hand to encourage the animal to turn in and around, using the whip now in your left hand to support this request. Immediately this begins to be complied with keep the movement going by using the whip to get the animal to walk away in a circle in the opposite direction. I use the command 'a-n-d HUP!' when doing this; it is normally soon learned and I get a smooth transition from a halt to a walk off in the opposite direction; later this is done at the walk without halting.

Do not expect things to go smoothly or progress with precise regularity as there are bound to be hitches even with the best animals; patience will eventually be rewarded. When quiet obedience is regular you can introduce some poles laid on the ground to walk and then to trot over when they are moved further apart. This will further strengthen the animal's body and its confidence in itself, and will also teach it to stride forwards better as the distance between the poles is gradually increased. Only use two poles at first, and do not place them beyond what you can see your particular horse or pony can achieve. As confidence and agility increase introduce a third pole and finally work up to four. An assistant may again be necessary at first to lead the young horse over the poles, but after the first time this should no longer be necessary. Later a small jump in the form of cavalletti can be added to 'pop' the horse or pony over, which will give variation to the routine and prepare for later work. As schooling continues the animal's outline will become longer and lower, with an extended neck and a noticeably relaxed and elastic back. With an improved outline brought about by the strengthened muscles the horse will begin to bring its hind legs further underneath for better engagement, and the forehand will raise and lighten as a result.

Greater collection on the lunge

Still alternating days of lungeing periods with fairly moderate riding in the open country, you can now direct the work on the lunge towards greater impulsion coupled with some collection. The horse or pony is tacked up with a snaffle bridle without a noseband, and the lungeing cavesson is fitted over the top with its straps buckled beneath the cheekstraps of the bridle. The snaffle bit can then be held loosely by the horse rather than its being clamped down by the cavesson. Saddle up the horse normally and either run up the stirrups or remove them altogether. Removal is sometimes better to begin with, as the sound and sensation of them bumping up and down on the saddle can unsettle and frighten a young horse. The snaffle rein can be laid across the pommel, or if the stirrups are left on and the rein is long enough it can be taken round under the stirrups in their run up position. After an initial period of lungeing in this extra 'dress', side reins are introduced to begin the work towards increased collection. These must be kept

As lungeing continues an easy, relaxed trot is obtained; the next stage will be to fit a bridle and side reins.

long at first to enable the horse or pony to walk freely with a natural carriage, and should be attached to the girth straps or the girth about level with the bottom of the saddle flap. Side reins with an elastic section to provide some give are desirable, as the horse will not feel restricted by a 'dead' rein. After working at the walk the side reins are shortened and trotting begun; shortening should at this stage be sufficient only to compensate for the naturally higher head carriage and narrower frame at the trot. After a period of trotting in both directions, finish up by allowing the horse to walk freely for ten minutes with loosened or removed side reins so it can return quietly to its stable with no stressful memories.

As work in these preliminary lessons on the lunge is continued the side reins must remain long enough to allow the young horse or pony freedom to stretch forwards and downwards to seek contact with the bit. It is most important to remember, however, that if they are too loose the animal will be unable to find this contact no matter how much it tries to do so. As the horse progresses, and continues to carry itself better with actively bent hindquarters producing a lively gait, the side reins can be shortened further, but they must still not be so tight that the horse finds it impossible to yield to them. It is also important to take the horse's lateral flexion on the circle into consideration, and to attach the outside side rein somewhat longer to allow for this. Elastic inserts in the side reins will help to some extent, but some compensation must still be made as the side reins are increasingly taken up. This essential adjustment is time-consuming as it must be done each time the horse changes direction.

Transition to canter

When training has progressed to a stage where the young horse or pony is carrying itself with poise, using the new-found suppleness of its hind legs and back in increased flexion and extension, the time has come to ask it for transition from trot to canter. With the horse trotting freely the trainer gives a slight pull on the lunge rein, momentarily bringing the horse slightly inside the path of the circle, and then yields immediately and at the same time uses the whip behind the animal in a driving control. At the same time I use the command 'g-a-lLOP'. (I find 'gallop' a better word for teaching a young horse than 'canter', but this is only a matter of personal choice.) Most horses or ponies 'released' in this manner will make the transition up to canter and naturally lead correctly with their inside leg. If they strike off wrongly, bring them back to the trot and try again. A correct response should again be rewarded with praise. Do not keep the canter going for too long, as it makes new demands on the animal's posture and will be tiring to perform. When asking for the change back to trot give a series of short tugs on the lunge to break the sequence and use the voice command. I call for the transition back to trot with the word 't-er-ROT'. Very soon you will find the animal comes to understand this action and will then come back to the trot on the voice command alone. If it tends to go mad at first when being asked to canter, do not tug at it violently or wave the whip about; merely remain calm and give it as much free lunge as possible until it quietens down of its own accord, when the trot can be obtained.

Do not try to teach too much too quickly, but allow all the new impressions to be absorbed by the horse or pony in the quietness of its stable between lessons. Alternating ridden work in the country with the work on the lunge will encourage the animal to use its back, especially when it is unhampered by a rider's weight, and will prevent it from becoming cramped or sagging from fatigue.

Long-reining

When the horse has learned to lunge properly and is responding to voice commands, a second lunge rein can be added and long-reining begun. The lungeing cavesson is used with the long reins fitted to each of the side rings and the trainer in position behind the animal. Do not stand up too close to start with in case the horse runs back or kicks out, but you need to be close enough to have control of the reins without a lot of slack. When the horse is at first asked to walk forwards it will probably be reluctant to do so, and it is helpful to have an assistant to walk at its shoulder to lead it forwards. Various methods can be used to guide each long rein along the animal's sides. The horse can be saddled, with the stirrup leathers fixed down by being joined under the girth by string or another strap; the long reins can then be passed through the leathers, which will guide them. Alternatively a surcingle can be used, with a crupper and side rings that have been fitted to the sides to act as guides for the reins. I personally prefer not to use

Long-reining from the bit must be 'kind' to the animal's mouth if the horse is to accept the trainer's hand controls willingly.

With the help of an assistant the trainer can encourage the horse forwards with greater activity and collection.

side attachments at the beginning, as with the reins free it is much easier to regain control (especially when working alone) if things go wrong and the horse manages to spin round and one rein goes over across its back. Once this happens horse and trainer will be face to face; if the reins are fitted through side attachments they will exert a backward pull on the animal, and the more it moves back the greater this pull becomes. To take the weight off the reins the trainer has to follow the horse as it backs away, and this of course encourages it to back more! On the other hand, if the reins are free they merely come straight forwards from the horse's head to the trainer, and the whole thing can be quickly sorted out.

Once the horse has settled down to walking on in front of the trainer, being guided around the schooling area by light but positive contact from the trainer's hands through the long reins to the sides of the cavesson, voice commands and gentle encouragement with the whip can obtain transitions from walk to trot, back to walk and halt. This entails some trotting along behind for the trainer, and helps to keep him or her fit as well! Soon, though, the animal can be allowed to go on alone and be brought round in a circle by the trainer moving inside and lengthening the outside rein. The horse will soon get accustomed to the feel of the second rein on its quarters as it moves in a large circle around the trainer as it did when lungeing. If trouble does occur it is usually because the trainer allows the outer rein to slip too low and tickle the horse's hocks; the animal will almost certainly object, so watch this point, especially with nervous animals.

Once you can work the horse in a large circle, changes in direction are brought about by the trainer moving sideways towards the rear of the circling horse and asking for the change in direction by manipulating the reins. This works in practice quite easily, and will come about naturally as horse and trainer progress. Once things are going satisfactorily with the horse working from a cavesson it can be replaced by a normal bridle with the long reins attached to the bit. Be sure that the bit is 'kind' and has a thick, comfortable mouthpiece. The trainer will now have direct contact with the animal's mouth and all movement must be kind and discreet to 'mouth' the horse and get it to accept the bit and respond to the trainer's hand controls. With the trainer using voice commands to which the animal is already accustomed, the combined result will be much smoother transitions, especially downwards, than was possible when lungeing from one rein. Practise transitions from walk to trot, so the horse can learn to accept guidance from the trainer's direct control on the bit without being burdened by the weight of a rider. If this is done properly, without roughness, the animal will soon learn to work without fear or hurrying and will gain a fair amount of collection and poise.

⑥ Elementary schooling

Up to now the young horse or pony has been ridden to strengthen and supple it and to get it going forwards under the rider's driving controls. This work has mainly been on straight lines, and any turns necessary have been taken when riding in open country with little real flexion. Now ridden work in the confines of a schooling arena must be begun so that circles with flexion can be brought about. A normal rectangle of not less than 40 by 20 metres should be used. At first do not ride into the corners; the horse should be allowed to come inside on a gentle curve at this stage of its training. The reason for this is that tight turns with a radius of three steps (as would be necessary if we rode right into the corners) would harm the gait and contact with the bit at this stage. Corners can only be ridden out properly after the young horse is responding positively to the driving controls while working on a circle. To bring this about we introduce some exercises that the horse or pony must learn to do without resistance before it is asked to perform a circle with flexion.

Turns on the forehand

An exercise that will strengthen the animal's understanding of and obedience to leg and rein controls is the turn on the forehand. At the start the hindquarters only make a partial circle, but as training progresses they make a full circle around the horse's inner foreleg after the animal has been brought to a halt. Begin by bringing the horse to a halt in the middle of the arena, and do not give up the reins when halting: the horse must momentarily stand still and calm before we proceed. To perform a left turn on the forehand (in which the hindquarters describe an arc to the right) proceed as follows. Increase the contact on the left rein by closing the fingers and withdrawing the left arm slightly; at the same time the left leg is placed distinctly behind the girth, pushing the hindquarters to the right. The rider's right hand maintains enough contact to prevent the horse's right shoulder from moving out or the horse

55

A left turn on the forehand in which the quarters describe an arc to the right. Contact with the left rein is increased by closing the fingers and withdrawing the arm slightly, while the left leg exerts pressure behind the girth to push the hindquarters to the right; the rider's pelvis also exerts sideways pressure to encourage the movement.

from moving forwards, and the rider's right leg remains at the girth to prevent the horse moving backwards. The rider also helps to induce the turn by a sideways pressure with his pelvis in the direction the hind legs will move, in this case to the right. The horse should pivot around its inner foreleg (in this case the left – near – foreleg) and its near hind leg steps inside and across the right – off – hind leg. The forelegs must not remain grounded and merely 'screw' round but must be picked up in a walking sequence. If the horse does not at first move across in response to the action of the rider's left leg the schooling whip or stick is used to reinforce the control until what is required is understood. Only describe a quarter circle to begin with, and when it has been achieved praise the horse and immediately walk it forwards. This is an excellent exercise for teaching the young horse or pony to respond to the lateral controls and yield to them. In turns on the forehand the animal's neck acts like a lever upon its body, compelling a mechanical action that brings about this yielding to the rider's leg control. To perform a right turn on the forehand the opposite to that described will obviously apply, and right turns should be practised alternately. After a few weeks these controls should be sufficiently well understood for a full circle to be achieved, revolving around the forehand with even loading on all four legs. As responsiveness continues to increase, have the animal walk forwards at any chosen point that you wish the turn to finish – sometimes describing a half circle, sometimes a full circle and so on – as this is very good for teaching immediate compliance to your leg controls.

Serpentines

These are ridden at the rising trot along the long side of the rectangular arena, and at first only single serpentines are ridden. The rising trot helps stimulate the young horse or pony to move forwards eagerly and so compensates for the natural loss of impulsion that the turning action creates. Keep the bends as flat as possible to begin with and straighten the horse for an instant before each turn. As collection improves and impulsion is maintained, double and then triple serpentines can be ridden, with more contact giving a more collected trot. Always endeavour to make the turns smooth and supple, using the driving leg controls together with the turning action of the reins. The rider must keep his legs in constant contact with the horse's sides and allow his upper body to follow the direction of the horse throughout the bends. If at first the young horse or pony does not understand what is required it can be performed at the walk until the animal is accustomed to the exercise, but trot as soon as possible because evasions are more easily learned at the walk.

Half halts

The half halt is an exercise that can be used to strengthen the hindquarters and get them used to carrying more weight with balance. While trotting actively on the rectangle of the schooling arena ask for a slow to walk, but immediately the horse slows yield with the hands and drive it forwards again with the legs. This exercise may be practised along one long side of the arena with serpentines along the other, and will activate the horse and improve its responsiveness. Do not overdo things so that the animal becomes bored or tired, but let it walk for a period on a long rein as a rest and reward when you feel it has worked willingly.

Circles at the trot

Anything from three to six months can elapse between the time you first begin to train a horse or pony in open country and the moment when this stage is reached. Sluggish animals will need longer to get them going forwards freely, whereas animals of a more impetuous nature can be started on the circle sooner. If earlier work, both ridden and on the lunge, has been carried out properly the horse will have no trouble in moving on a curved line. It will adapt its body to the circle with increasing amounts of flexion so that its inner side becomes concave – bending around the rider's inside leg – and its outer side convex, held in position, as it were, by the opposing effect of the rider's outside leg. The rider's shoulders should follow the direction of the circle in line with the horse's shoulders and with a slightly shortened inner rein. If the tension felt on both reins is approximately the same the horse will be moving around the circle with correct flexion. Corresponding to this flexion and depending on the circumference and rate of the circle being ridden, the horse's centre of gravity will move inwards, and the rider's seat adapts to this. Because of this shift of gravity, the animal's inside hind leg will now be burdened with the task of increased weight carrying, and the joints will be called upon to bend more vigorously. The outside hind leg, relieved of some of its burden, will be better able to travel forwards the greater distance that is necessary to maintain the flexion on the circle. The horse is kept exactly on the circle by its hindquarters being guided and controlled by the rider's legs and its forehand by his hands, and the more the animal supples in longitudinal flexion the more easily will the rider's inside leg maintain the concave bend. The rider's inside leg must remain clinging to the horse's body just behind the girth, where it maintains the concave bend of the horse and prevents the horse from moving towards the centre of the circle. When coming off the circle to proceed straight along the long side of the arena it acts with the reins to lead the horse off the circle. The outer side of the horse is controlled by the rider's outside leg, which automatically positions itself somewhat further behind the girth. From this position it acts as a driving agent to the outer hind leg, encouraging the necessarily longer stride, and also prevents the quarters from swinging off the track. In this position the rider's outside leg also aids the inner rein, which keeps the horse's head turned slightly inwards, harmonizing the entire length of the horse in longitudinal flexion around the circle.

Lateral flexion comes by the spine bending from the mid-point forwards, through the dorsal vertebrae to the neck. Behind the saddle the vertebrae through the pelvic region to the tail are laterally inflexible, and 'bend' here is produced by a lengthening and shortening of the muscles on either side of the horse.

These explanations of turns on the forehand and circles in either direction will have shown that the combined action of the rider's inside leg and outside rein, and vice versa, gives him 'diagonal control' whereas the controls that act on the same side of the horse provide his 'lateral control'.

As the horse progresses, smaller circles can gradually be ridden

58

Serpentines and circles at the trot must be ridden with maintained impulsion, and if this suffers the horse must be taken off the circle and worked in a straight line to re-establish an eagerness to go forwards.

by taking the horse round in a decreasing circle and then immediately pushing it out into the larger circle again. The rider must never allow his restraining outer hand to cross the withers even though the rein is brought against the animal's neck, as if he does its action will no longer be felt by the horse's hind leg on that side. The rider's hands remain at all times in position on their own side of the neck. If gait and impulsion start to suffer while working on the circle, or if the hindquarters evade by stepping inside the circle track, the horse must be taken off and worked in a straight line to re-establish even loading and eagerness to go forwards. As soon as the horse is responding well on the circle it can be ridden into the corners of the arena more closely when working around the school. If, however, this upsets its timing or makes the gait hurried and less expressive we take the corner less closely until the horse has developed the strength and poise to carry itself better. When bringing the horse off a circle to go along a straight line the inner rein yields and the horse responds by accepting the outside rein again.

The rising trot

The rider will use the rising trot to take the weight off the horse's back and so help its back and hindquarters to bend and stretch to the track of the circle. He must not, however, rise out of the saddle more than the impulse of the motion demands or impulsion will be lost; likewise he must not push his buttocks to the rear or allow his back to collapse or assume too much of a forward angle or the

59

drive as he is seated at every second step will be lost. The rider's knees and ankles must be kept supple and allow his legs to lie close to the horse's body and follow the rhythm of the trot.

There is considerable conflict about which diagonals the rider should rise on when performing the rising trot (or posting, as it is known in the USA), and which hind leg should carry the load as the rider sits. I am sure that many riders are confused on this point. I will therefore give my own simple explanation of my preference and why I favour it. I think it best for the rider to be seated in the saddle as the outside foreleg of the animal is grounded when riding a rectangle or circle. As the diagonals of the horse work together at the trot, giving a two-time pace, this means the rider is also seated as the inside hind leg is in contact with the ground and taking the weight. The rider's weight in the saddle as the inside hind leg is grounded encourages it to accept the load and bend in active impulsion for the thrust off. The centre of gravity moves slightly to the inside while the horse is trotting a circle, and the weight is more naturally balanced if the rider is seated on the inner hind leg; at the same time it will free the outer hind leg and thereby encourage that leg to travel further forwards, as it must do on the horse's 'long' convex side on the outer curve of the circle.

A rising trot, with the rider maintaining impulsion by not rising too high or allowing the back to collapse; legs are in perfect contact and the ankles are supple. Note that the rider will be seated as the inner hind leg comes to the ground to take up the weight.

A quick glance will immediately tell you which diagonal you are on. To be seated on the inside hind leg you will see the horse's outside shoulder stretched forwards as you are at the top of your rise just before you start the downward movement. As you sit, that shoulder moves back as the outside foreleg and inside hind leg come to the ground. A word of warning here – never look down by tilting your head forwards, as this will affect your whole balance (as explained in chapter 3). It is no good, however, to tell the rider that not even a glance is permissible and that he must be able to feel which diagonal he is on, as this will be beyond all except the very advanced rider. When working at the rising trot in open country the diagonals on which you sit should be changed at regular intervals of five minutes or so in order to strengthen the muscles of the hind legs evenly and not continually burden only the one. With even development of the muscles, ligaments and joints on both sides by riding in this manner you will also help to avoid crookedness.

Beginning work on two tracks

About three or four months after work on a circle has begun the young horse or pony will have gained sufficient strength and flexion to begin work on two tracks. This earlier work should have resulted in the animal responding to the rider's leg – leg yielding – without its eagerness or gait suffering. The riding of curved lines, half and full halts should also have gradually encouraged a fair amount of collection while in positive contact with the bit. When beginning work on two tracks the rider must not use force to achieve his objective, nor can the exercise be done if the horse or pony holds its head too high, hollowing and stiffening its back.

The best way to start two-track work is with the left and right shoulder-in movement, which must be derived from the normal trot with more thrust developed from the hindquarters; this increased impulsion is controlled by the rider's hands and the small of his back, and as a result the force is redirected back to the joints of the stifle and hocks, rather like compressing a spring. With the cooperation of the horse's back the animal will begin to develop a powerful thrust with the hind legs before they are fully extended, and consequently leave the ground from an already bent position. This enables the forelegs to be raised freely in a smooth, rhythmic action. The line of the horse's face towards the nose should be slightly ahead of the vertical with the poll nicely flexed to allow the movement to flow elastically through its body. At first it is best to practise this trot for a few weeks, being satisfied by a few loftier steps to begin with and gradually increasing the demands until it can be maintained for two complete circuits of the schooling arena. There must be a relative lifting of the forehand through a higher

Trotting over poles to encourage a loftier step and a powerful thrust from the hindquarters before they are fully extended. The rider rises higher for this exercise to allow the horse's back and quarters greater freedom to pulsate forwards.

carriage of head and neck as a consequence of the lowering of the hindquarters. If the horse cannot maintain its timing and becomes stiff to the seat and hands it must be given more time to meet the demands of a collected gait. A dragging of the hindquarters, the loss of positive contact with the bit or hasty and uneven steps means that too much has been attempted and the rider must allow the horse to return to the comparative freedom of the former trot for a period in order to restore gait and contact. There is always the danger, too, of overtaxing a horse or pony that is willing and possesses natural animation by working it to overtiredness, when it will lose the correct tension of the more or less collected gait and then fall apart. This will result in the forelegs failing to advance in time and remaining grounded for too long; the hind legs will 'catch them up' and cause overreaching. Horses that are responsive and willing can so enthuse and delight the rider that he may unwittingly go on for too long. It should always be remembered that waiting for the horse to mature fully will result in its having a much longer useful life. Horses that possess a high degree of energy, which enables them to work with seemingly inexhaustible reserves of power, when back in their stables will often show signs of exhaustion, such as refusing food or breaking out in a cold sweat after having cooled off. If this happens repeatedly then the rider is at fault – the remedy is obvious.

62

Shoulder-in

Shoulder-in is best developed by trotting around the arena until reaching the corner that leads into the long side of the school. Coming out of the corner, the rider momentarily leads the horse or pony off the track using both reins as though starting a circle, but instead his inside leg, acting at the girth, pushes the animal's forehand forwards along the long side. The bend the horse has assumed in starting the circle is maintained as it is pushed forwards

To begin shoulder-in work the horse is momentarily led off the track after coming out of a corner, as though continuing a circle; the rider's inside leg then pushes the forehand forwards along the long side, causing the inside hind leg to follow the line of the outside foreleg.

along the long side of the school and this causes the inside hind leg to follow the line made by the outside foreleg. To maintain this position the rider's outside leg is brought back behind the girth to prevent the quarters from swinging outwards. The horse must not be allowed just to bend its neck but must be flexed at the ribs, the rider's inside leg being the centre pivot of the curve. The rider's inside leg will also act to drive the horse forwards in this position should it hold back. Each rein has a special job to do as the horse is led into the shoulder-in; the inside rein is somewhat shortened, supporting the curve around the rider's inside leg; the outside rein prevents the neck from overbending and maintains the shoulder along the given line. After a few steps have been completed, or if the horse loosens its neck, it is driven forwards towards the centre of the arena, maintaining the curve but with the pressure of the rider's inside leg relaxed to allow the horse to go forwards in a large half circle. This is better than bringing the horse back onto the outside track, as it is already bent in the direction of the circle and it is therefore easier for it to continue this way. Each week a few more steps at shoulder-in are asked for until the animal can eventually perform this exercise for the entire length of the long side of the arena – in both directions, of course.

As in all two-track work, it must be borne in mind that a few powerful, expressive steps at shoulder-in are more than enough at first; the young horse or pony must subsequently be allowed to stretch its joints by going on to perform some free gaits. If the rider tries to persist for too long in collected lateral flexion it will overload the joints, which will quickly lose their springy elasticity. As work progresses the degree of shoulder-in can be increased so the horse is moving on two different tracks, the hind legs following one track and the forelegs on a track parallel to them. This will call for greater flexibility at the horse's ribs and more active hind legs.

The canter

I have already explained why the young horse or pony should not be cantered in the schooling arena too soon: it will not be able to balance itself properly. Forcing it to canter would only give it a distaste for the gait and produce tensions at every canter attempt. As work continues, however, we need not suppress a spontaneously offered canter and can let the horse break into a working canter at an opportune moment. With spirited young animals that long to canter and need to let off steam from time to time, it is best to let them do so in open country where straight lines can be cantered. Trying to restrain such horses will only tend to make them 'explode', and the struggle will do more harm to the mouth than will be caused to joints and ligaments in youthful forward capers. Out in the country we can let the horse find its

Perfect harmony of horse and rider in a classical example of a fluid, long-striding working trot. The forward impulsion produced from the quarters can be seen travelling through the back right up to the poll as the rider sits in perfect rhythm (Chapter 1). (Photo: Margaret Elliot)

A nice unhurried walk with calmness and poise. The horse is being encouraged to lengthen its stride and walk forwards into the bit (Chapters 3 and 4).

A balanced rising trot with even loading on all four legs. The two-time gait can be clearly seen with the diagonals acting together, in this case the near fore and off hind being grounded with the opposite diagonals airborne.

Snowy conditions often give rise to high spirits in horses, who react to the atmospheric conditions by becoming more than usually excitable. Here horse and rider enjoy a rather bouncy canter that shows the tremendous power produced by the horse's quarters.

In the cold winds of winter exercise and training must go on, and for those without indoor facilities or an all-weather schooling arena the open country will have to suffice.

Canter half pass to the left showing the middle beat of the three phases, with the centre of gravity moving sideways and forwards with the rider's weight correctly leading the movement.

Accelerating to a gallop in the confines of a small arena exerts tremendous forces on the tendons, ligaments and joints. Only mature, fit horses with iron-hard legs should be asked to do this exercise.

A collected trot showing perfect cadence and poise, with both horse and rider in classical outline. Patience and progressive training over many months are needed to bring a horse to this stage of collection while still maintaining expressive impulsion (Chapter 8).

A rising trot with horse and rider and nicely balanced showing the rider seated on the inner hind and outer fore diagonals. The rider has a good head, hands, seat and leg position with the horse going forwards with impulsion into the bit (Chapter 6).

Energetic passage*: here the author demonstrates how riding with one hand can 'release' the horse and enable the rider's seat to 'melt' into the saddle. Note too how the rider's body remains relaxed but upright (Chapters 3 and 9).*

Long-reining in Andalusia: this 20-year-old stallion is brought back from an active passage to commence piaffe. *Note how the horse is engaging its hocks deeply, bringing its centre of gravity back towards the haunches (Chapters 5 and 9).*

Flying changes Spanish style. Champion vaquero *rider Don Rafael Jurado performs flying changes with his Andalusian stallion while circling his stable yard.*

Half pass to the left: the horse is slightly bent around the rider's left leg, freeing its right shoulder which allows it to step firmly across with the diagonals acting together (Chapter 9).

balance at the canter with a free posture and reins not too constrained, as we did to begin with in the natural trot. Try to let these free canters occur on slightly rising or at least level ground, as the horse will not be ready to balance itself cantering downhill. Even more dangerous is a sharp downhill stretch immediately followed by an uphill one, especially on wet ground as the animal will 'lose its legs' in the dip. It is always wise even with a mature horse not to let it gallop into wet ground where it may flounder, but to look ahead and check its speed momentarily before the dip is reached. Picking one's place with a young and exuberant horse will teach it that the canter is not something to get over-excited about but is like any other gait and produced at the demand of the rider. This will prepare it for when it is first allowed to canter a large rectangle in the confines of the schooling arena.

Now our young mount is able to work in the school at a shortened working trot and can obey the rider's lateral controls it is time to progress to a correct canter on a large circle (or more correctly an elliptic rectangle). Begin by riding around the arena at a shortened working trot, because this will make it easier for the horse to make the transition to canter when the time comes.

As the horse starts coming through the corner leading along the long side of the arena the rider, whose inner seat bone is carrying more load, draws back his outside leg behind the girth, sits deep and applies strong pressure with *both* legs. The precise moment for the canter will be as the horse's forehand is about to straighten to go along the long side and its ribs are still flexed with the quarters still curved slightly on the bend. This will break the trot sequence and the horse should automatically strike off into a correct canter with its inside foreleg leading. Only light contact with the bit is maintained in this early training and the canter should be long, without collection. After half a circuit the horse can be brought back to a trot by the rider bracing his back and slightly resisting with the hands. Then the horse is walked on and congratulated.

There is a great deal of controversy about the precise form the use of the rider's leg controls should take for a transition to canter so I will explain in detail the reasons for the controls I advocate. The canter is a beat of three-time, with the horse's 'laterals' acting together – the inside foreleg and inside hind leg slightly advanced from their opposite counterparts on the outside when cantering a circle. (Hence we ask for the transition to canter coming out of a corner with the horse slightly bent, when its inside foreleg will naturally lead.) The canter phase sequence is as follows: (1) outside hindleg, (2) inside hind leg and outside foreleg, (3) inside foreleg, followed by a period of 'flying' with all four legs in the air until the outside hind leg takes up the sequence again. The outside hind leg is thus the one that takes the initial load as it is grounded, and in the correct canter exerts the initial thrust to propel the animal forwards. For this reason the rider's outside leg must be drawn back to just behind the girth and strong pressure applied to ask the horse to accept the load and thrust off into canter, and at the same time the rider's inside leg applies strong pressure in its position at the girth to make the horse's inside hind leg sustain this forward thrust as it takes over the load. It is most important that the rider uses *both* legs, as if he does not – and gets the horse to canter by merely drawing back his outside leg – he will experience trouble later on when asking for lateral work such as the half-pass when the horse will depart in canter. This method is mostly agreed on by the pundits; where they differ is in the degree of strength that each of the rider's legs employs – whether each should effect the same pressure, or whether the inside or the outside leg should be the stronger. I advocate strong pressure from both the rider's legs acting together, but with a slightly stronger pressure from his outside leg. There are two reasons for this; first it encourages the horse to strike off with its outside hind leg into the canter and at the same time to reach forwards with the diagonal inner foreleg, thus correctly leading with it; second, the slight extra pressure from the rider's outside leg automatically places his pelvis deeper, with an increased shift of his weight to the inner side, helping the horse's outer hind leg as it thrusts off. Another reason for using this method of leg control for transition to canter is that it is easier for the horse to learn which leg is being asked for – left canter or right canter – when departing in a straight line rather than on a circle.

When transitions to canter do not go as smoothly as desired and the horse or pony becomes excited, keep the driving controls in contact with it and if possible refrain from fighting with the animal's mouth. This will help the rider to keep a strong seat and calm the horse. When composure is restored, stroke the animal's neck and generally quieten it down before asking for canter again. With a horse that is at first reluctant to canter (assuming that it has had sufficient preliminary training), give a click of the tongue as the controls are given and also a slight tap on its inside shoulder with the whip. On no account must the rider allow his back to 'collapse' when asking for canter, as this will cause his seat to be ineffective. Once the canter is achieved do not sustain constant leg pressure but relax and go along with the movement. Then bring the horse back to trot again by closing the legs, bracing the back and providing the necessary restraint with the reins. Always remember to shorten the trot before going into canter, and do try not to let the horse 'run' into it. Practise transitions back to trot until the horse can do this without resistance or throwing up its head. Finally, do not always use the same place in the arena to ask for canter as the horse will then anticipate your controls and not 'listen'; practice should of course be given equally in canters to the right and to the left.

7 Learning to jump

Most young horses and ponies show a natural tendency to jump. Provided that they are not over-fenced, there is no reason why they should not be allowed to 'pop' over small natural obstacles in the open country once they can carry themselves and their rider with confidence. By this I do not mean that they should be ridden hell-bent at fences or hedges, but that small fallen tree trunks across bridle paths and the like can be trotted up to and quietly jumped. Later the canter can also be used on approach. At both gaits the rider must keep impulsion going so that the animal realizes what is expected of it and does not stop short because of the rider's failure to ride it forwards at the obstacle. Many people, not having access to a schooling area, will have to use the open country for teaching their horse to jump if it is later to take part in competitions or hunting. The horse's training programme should in any case include work in rough country, with progressively more hilly work as it grows stronger.

What was stated earlier about the risk of damage to young joints and ligaments is doubly true when jumping obstacles, and I would strongly advise against jumping a horse seriously until it is at least six years old. There is also a risk of the horse injuring itself when jumping (such as overreaching on landing), which is much more likely when a horse is immature or tired. In order to combat such injuries owners often use protective guards or boots made of leather or plastic, of which there are many different types. These can be very effective, but I must say that I feel many people resort to them because of persuasive advertising or because it is fashionable and they like to see their animal 'dressed' in some additional clutter. For myself, unless the horse shows a tendency to this type of injury I do not like to use them, preferring to rely on systematic training to strengthen the horse. However, for those who feel happier using protective equipment for the animal's legs, there is no reason I can give for them not to do so except to say that their use does not compensate for overtaxing a young animal's strength and fitness.

When first teaching the young horse to jump use a low obstacle; the rider must go forwards with the animal, allowing it to stretch its back and find its balance.

Schooling over obstacles

Elementary training over obstacles for the schooled horse or pony in an enclosed arena will begin with cavalletti, or a similar arrangement with poles, to form a low jump. The horse will already be familiar with the trotting poles, which are used while working on the lunge, and it is a good idea to extend this work with the animal trotting over poles while ridden. This helps the horse to balance itself and adapt to the changing centre of gravity. It will also learn to lengthen its stride if the poles are placed on the ground a little further apart than the normal trotting stride; placing them a little closer together and raised about 9 in (20 cm) at one end will make the horse bend and lift its hind legs in greater engagement. For these trotting exercises the number of poles can gradually be increased until five or six are spread out, about 5 ft (1.5 m) apart depending on the size and stride of the animal. If the horse 'hops' out over the last two or puts in an extra step the poles need to be brought closer together. If the poles are set up too high the animal will be obliged to hop with its hind legs instead of trotting. If the animal is nervous or unsure of what it is meant to do, let it first have a good look and then walk over the poles, and you will not have any further trouble.

When the young horse or pony is first jumped over low cavalletti the rider must allow the reins total freedom except for direction, as the young animal must feel completely free to stretch its neck and head forwards and downwards. This is necessary for it to take a good look and also to learn to stretch its back and entire body. This freedom will also allow it to find, by its own efforts, the new balance required, at this stage only helped by the rider by his going with the movement and not being 'left behind'.

Working at the trot, the height of the obstacles should be 12 to 18 in (30 to 45 cm) so that the animal is obliged to jump and not just to trot across them. When adding another jump, place it at a distance of about 9 ft (2.7 m) from the first, according to the animal's length of stride. The rider must now concentrate on his own style by keeping his head high, looking straight ahead not down; and his knees must act as a fixed fulcrum to support and balance his own weight in rhythm with the moving centre of gravity. This is most important and best achieved if the rider shortens his stirrups by about two holes so that his weight can more readily be lifted from the saddle; at the same time his knees and lower legs should remain in position to support his seat and absorb the shock when landing. After some time, depending on the horse's ability, jumping low obstacles at the canter will begin. This will start to prepare the horse for higher obstacles, as it must assume the posture that is required for jumping these as well. Use a single jump about 18 in (45 cm) high to begin with; when this can be taken smoothly at the canter add another approximately 18 ft (5.4 m) away. Later still, add a third obstacle at 36 ft (10.8 m) from the first. These are set up to correspond to the animal's canter stride, so it may be necessary to increase or decrease the distances given depending on the size and the stride of the horse. Care must be taken not to overtire the young horse; it must not be continually jumped until fatigue causes it to refuse or run out, or to injure itself. None of these things is likely to happen if we finish before the animal has become tired or bored with the exercise.

After a few weeks, depending on progress, two low jumps can be placed about 8 ft (2.4 m) apart and then jumped without an intermediate canter stride in between; two obstacles placed close together will also make a single jump of additional width to provide a small 'spread' fence. The loosening and stretching effect of this work over low obstacles will be very advantageous in preparing the young horse for the more strenuous work of steep climbing or steep descending in open country, as well as for future jumping over larger obstacles. It will also be of great benefit to the animal, even if it is intended principally for dressage, by freeing its back and getting rid of unwanted tensions. (To this end it is always a good idea to have a small jump handy when doing dressage training to use as a reward and welcome break from working in collection, and to stretch and loosen the animal's muscles.)

Progress to higher jumps

For horses or ponies intended for use in events and competitions involving jumping, larger and more solid obstacles must be introduced. This is best done out of doors or out in the country where they can be built 'naturally'. Solid jumps between 2 and 3 ft high (60 to 90 cm) will be needed, and these should be kept fairly narrow with bushes or upright branches on either side. Jumps made from logs and tree branches are good, as these natural materials encourage the animal to jump rather than frighten it. When being constructed these will need to have a 'ground line' to help the horse judge its distance at takeoff. A pole or log on the ground some 2 or 3 ft (60 to 90 cm) in front of the jump will do this, or the jump can be built in such a way that it slopes upwards, giving the horse an inviting lead into it. 'Wings' on either side should also be added, and the whole thing given a solid appearance so that the horse knows it must jump. With the wings leading into the obstacle the horse is less likely to be tempted to run out; this leading in to a narrow obstacle also teaches the horse to jump straight and not at an angle.

Before the jump is attempted for the first time, walk the animal up to it so that it can sniff it and take a good look in order to overcome any fear of its strangeness. Trotting the horse at first to jump the obstacle at its lowest height will help some animals to judge their stride better, but enough impulsion must be maintained or the horse will refuse. If the horse shifts into a canter by itself as it approaches, the rider should adapt to this gait and allow the horse to go forwards in this way. As jump training continues the canter will be used deliberately and the rider will regulate this either by driving the horse forwards when it becomes hesitant or by restraining a headlong dash if the animal is impetuous; the rider's legs and back always play an important part in supervising these demands. We have probably all witnessed riders who thump with their legs or 'snatch' with their hands when approaching a jump or at takeoff, and it may be that some riders with certain problem horses feel obliged to use methods of this kind. However, I believe the best assistance one can render the horse when jumping is to relieve the load on its hindquarters by use of the forward jumping seat. This also enables the rider to help the horse use its neck as a balancing rod as it 'dives'. The trainer's job is to give the horse systematic progressive training to strengthen its muscles and joints, thus preparing its hindquarters, back and neck for the greater physical exertions required when jumping larger obstacles. If the earlier work has been properly done and gradually advanced, the horse will have developed its gymnastic skill and jumping technique. The actual jumping mechanism, whereby the levers of the horse's frame are activated by muscular effort to

As training continues and the height of the jump increases, the rider must relieve the load and help the horse to use its neck as a balancing rod as it 'dives'.

enable it to negotiate an obstacle, must be left to the horse itself to organize.

With larger jumps, calling for greater impulsion or more speed at takeoff, the horse will find it harder to judge the takeoff correctly, and this will only come after considerable experience over all types of jump. With low jumps the takeoff distance is fairly easy for the horse to judge, and it can get over with a flat trajectory even if it takes off too early. As the height of the jump increases, so must the horse's trajectory become higher and more arched, and the point of takeoff is more critical for a successful jump. To help the horse find its distance for takeoff over higher obstacles, place a lower jump in front, one canter stride away. To encourage the horse to arch its back and neck when jumping, set up a jump that cannot be seen through, such as one made from solid planking, and place a lower jump just beyond it that the horse only sees at the moment of takeoff. The effect of this will be to make the horse assume an arched, diving outline during its flight. This can be further modified by placing another low fence just in front

71

of the solid one, which will make for proper takeoff and a nice arched extension as the horse jumps. The jumps most difficult for the horse to judge are high upright fences with no ground line, and these should not be attempted until the animal has gained experience and is in much more advanced stages of its training.

Jumping with confidence and style

To jump higher obstacles – say those over 3 ft (1 m) – the rider will probably need to use a special jumping saddle, rather than the

With larger jumps the horse's trajectory becomes higher and more arched; the rider uses the forward jumping seat with his knees acting as a fixed fulcrum to support and balance his own weight in rhythm with that of the horse. The rider's head is held high and looking straight ahead, and his sympathetic hands are ready to release the horse as it dives over the jump, stretching its neck for balance.

general purpose or working saddle that sufficed before. Saddles designed for jumping have the knee supports extended so the rider can shorten his stirrups by four holes or so and still have his knees properly supported. Saddles not properly shaped would fail to achieve this, and also place the rider's legs and knees in the wrong position. A good jumping saddle will provide the support necessary for the rider to lift his body from the pivot of his more forward knee position after using his driving seat control; it will then allow him to keep his back flat and give the horse's neck maximum freedom over the jump. The rider's upper body, hinged at the knee, must follow the horse's movement over the jump from the moment of takeoff and not be 'left behind', which causes interference to the animal. The rider must approach each jump confident that the horse will jump successfully, and this confidence will be transmitted to the animal. Any doubt on the rider's part will be communicated to the horse, whose instincts will tell it that if the rider has doubts it should too; a mess of some kind will probably result. The success of many riders is due to their confidence and allows many to adopt styles of their own that defy tradition. However, while the average rider will do well to show confidence in his mount when jumping, he should refrain from trying to copy the unorthodox styles of some leading riders.

If your horse shows an aptitude for jumping and you intend to pursue this, don't exploit its talent by consistently trying to find out how high it can jump. Take the animal through each stage of its training with patience. Eventually, when it can jump say 4 ft (1.3 m), be satisfied with entering it in a competition where the average height is somewhat less. Only after the horse can jump this height in training over all types of fences and obstacles should it be asked to jump them in competition. When a horse refuses a jump it is a sign that you have asked it to negotiate the higher obstacle too soon, or have presented it with a different type of fence that again is too big. The answer is to go back to a lower one again to restore its confidence.

Another aspect of later training is to give the horse a gallop once a week to sharpen it up. This is especially helpful for animals that tend to sulk or become uncertain through no fault of the trainer. Such horses may become disobedient and come to a stop when asked to jump, and the rider will then have to resort to vigorous use of his buttocks, remaining in the saddle, until takeoff is achieved. Refusals and run-outs must never be left; when they occur they must be followed by a successful jump, even if this has to be over a lower obstacle. Rushing at the jump is another fault that may be caused by fear or nervousness; calming the horse over a low jump before approaching several higher ones spaced at different intervals will often make it less impetuous. But if the horse's fear is due not to the actual jump but to the painful jerk it feels in the mouth or blows on the back from a clumsy rider, changing the rider will identify the problem. If no such problems occur with the new rider, the lesson must be learned and the mistakes corrected. Lastly, the horse has a very keen sense of smell and will know when the rider is afraid because of the odour that all creatures – human and animal – emit when they are frightened. It is imperceptible to humans, but horses instantly notice it, and their logic will then make them unsure and disobedient. This can be another reason why one rider will get more from a horse when jumping than another.

Making your own practice jumps

Small cavalletti or practice jumps need not be expensive manufactured ones. Small poles of some 8 ft (2.5 m) in length and 3 or 4 in (8 to 10 cm) diameter, placed on upturned rubber buckets, will serve as jumps. They need not be wider than this, but do not have them much narrower; if you do, say to 5 ft 6 in (1.75 m), then place some 'dolls' on either side to lead the horse into the low obstacle – this will help to prevent it from diving out to the side.

For those readers who can use a hammer and saw I will explain how I made my own schooling jumps from scrap materials at

The author's home-made jumps with the 'wings' in position. The ground poles can be moved further out to encourage the horse to take off early.

Close-up of the fittings, which allow the poles to revolve.

practically no cost at all. I visited my local scrap merchant and was lucky to find a dozen or so wooden rollers that had been scrapped from an old laundry or mill. They were 7 ft (2.2 m) long, 4 in (10 cm) in diameter, and to my delight had solid steel rods through the middle and protruding 1¼ in (3 cm) at each end. I bought them for a song as no one could imagine a use for them, and then used some odd pieces of wood to make some small stands. By fixing some hardwood blocks at intervals on the stand uprights (first providing these blocks with cut-outs), I had an adjustable set of jumps. Most pleasing was the fact that the steel rods made the poles heavy enough not to bounce out of the slots easily, and if they were struck by the horse's hoof they could revolve in the end 'cups'. The illustrations plainly show the principle, which can be copied by anyone who can acquire similar materials.

8 More advanced training

Rarely, if ever, will you be lucky enough to work with a horse or pony that progresses smoothly in its training and presents no difficulties through faulty conformation, temperament or disposition. The best progress will be made by the rider and trainer who is prepared to accept a long period of training, and to advance only according to the horse's own progress. However, difficulties will still arise, and what can be achieved on one day will be unattainable, or at best sporadic, on the next. Don't let this worry you too much, as this somewhat erratic progress will gradually level out to a more consistent and precise achievement.

When the young horse or pony has completed its elementary training and can be taken through its ridden work with consistent performance, and has consequently obtained the necessary suppleness of its hindquarters and joints, we can proceed to the stage of training that will demand greater concentration and effort from the animal. Now that the animal has been systematically prepared for advancement, greater collection will be asked for by the rider. The corners of the schooling arena will now be ridden into, and turns and circles made smaller to correspond to the animal's increased suppleness.

Collection

Increased collection can only be properly obtained when the earlier training has suppled and strengthened the hindquarters sufficiently for the rider to place a heavier burden upon them. The conformation and aptitude of the horse will govern the length of time that has to be allowed before embarking on this stage of its education. Even with animals suitably endowed, however, it should not be attempted before the second year of training, and it is often necessary to delay much longer than this. True collection is the attainment of vigorous and expressive strides produced from a pulsating back and lowered hindquarters. This produces the pleasing outline of a compact framework with the neck extended forward and upward. The head is held with poise, from the heightened poll through a vertical or near-vertical face to where the mouth accepts the bit with a relaxed chewing that produces saliva. Together with this bodily collection comes an increased attentiveness and a readiness to obey the rider's controls instantly without evasion or intractability. Any rider or trainer who can bring about this state of readiness will reap the highest reward. To achieve this level of understanding and cooperation the horse's early training must be thorough and unhurried, and the rider's controls consistent and clear throughout the training period.

Refining the controls

To achieve collection the rider, by use of his legs, must drive the horse forwards more actively, causing its hind legs to push off more forcefully and engage further forwards. This will produce an energetic rhythm, with the animal's muscles flexing and relaxing in harmony with the movement. As the horse stretches out to the bit, its back and entire spinal length from the croup to the poll will stretch to form the correct arch and so fill out the rider's seat. From this position the rider's seat can follow the movement of the horse and also act to drive it forwards, so the hind legs bend and stretch even farther forwards and spring off the ground with even more energy. This vigorous but supple locomotion is the basis of collection; the hind legs step longer and livelier, passing each other more closely and with this impulsion accepting a larger share of the load. This will give a relative lift to the forehand, with increased freedom of movement from the shoulders. Now the rider can use the driving force of his back and seat to maintain impulsion while his hands passively sustain the increased impulsion ready to convert it into greater collection. The reins will become slacker as a result of the lifted arching of the neck, and the rider shortens these to a passive contact with the horse's mouth. This contact must maintain an even pressure, yielding somewhat rather than exerting a continuous backward pull. Only when the animal tries to shift the load from its hindquarters to the forehand should brief pulls on the reins be used, and these must cease as soon as the forehand lightens and the load is once again moved onto the hind legs. If the rider fails to do this and instead exerts a continued pull on the reins, the horse will shorten the stride of its hind legs and adopt a faulty gait. Similarly, the horse will hurry with shortened strides if the rider's legs continue forcibly to drive the horse forwards while the reins are being tugged. For this reason the rider must only use his legs vigorously when the animal's hind legs are not engaging effectively and are being 'left behind'. As soon as the horse responds by bringing its hind legs underneath to take the weight, the rider's legs should remain clinging gently to the sides of the horse, allowing his weight to be carried along in harmony with the movement. If the increased drive is maintained for too long after the horse has responded, the opposite of what was required will result: the horse will stiffen its back and cause its hindquarters to drag. The rider must thus become tuned to his horse to obtain and maintain collection; when the feel from the horse's mouth becomes 'dead' and impulsion begins to fade the rider's legs must reawaken the horse. If the animal starts to bore on the bit and hurries forwards, the rider's hands must adjust the gait by brief pulls on the reins supported by the small of his back to make the horse shift the load back onto its hind legs. As collection increases to the ultimate dressage collection the rider will feel the centre of gravity shift towards the lowered hindquarters; expressive, positive steps with freedom and poise will be seen by the trainer; the suppleness of the horse's back together with its shortened outline will allow the rider's seat to melt into the saddle and his legs to follow smoothly the movement of the horse. From this state the attentiveness of the horse will be such that any command for a change of rate, direction or gait will be instantly obeyed. In short, the rider and horse are as one.

The conformation, ability and natural talent of both horse and rider will dictate the degree of collection obtainable. Judgement must be used to recognize the limit of collection possible for a particular horse, and the rider should feel satisfied when this has been achieved. Both horse and rider will be able to maintain the improved poise and posture in their normal work in the schooling arena and in open country.

Collected trot

Begin this exercise by first warming the horse into a working trot, then shorten this pace for several steps along the long side of the arena before allowing it to proceed forwards in the working trot once more. These transitions from working trot to a shortened trot and vice versa will gradually bring about the increased springiness of the joints of the hindquarters that is essential for collected work. As the animal responds to the rider's controls, and alternately stretches out to the working trot and bends in greater collection for the shortened strides, its impulsion will increase and the hindquarters will carry more of the load. This will bring about an automatic progression to a collected trot, and the rider can now concentrate on trying to attain loftier and more expressive steps from this newly acquired collection. Be careful not to overdo this at first, and when you feel the response has been given continue it only for a short distance, and immediately reward the horse by riding it forwards in a freer gait and give it an encouraging word and a pat. The horse must also be ridden forwards vigorously to

For a collected trot the rider, seated deep in the saddle, uses the leg controls to drive the horse forwards, then maintains impulsion using seat and back while the hands passively shorten the reins.

improve its gait if it loses its timing or the former lofty steps lose their liveliness and become flat. Contact with the bit and a free, pulsating back will be brought about by this riding forwards, and must be achieved before attempting an expressive collected trot once more. If trouble is experienced by the horse leaning on the bit when a collected trot is performed, the light tugs on the reins followed by increased activation of the hind legs described earlier should restore the correct position. As work progresses and the horse is asked to pass from a walk to a trot or to trot forwards from a halt, the rider must ensure that his controls are answered by pure trotting steps.

Extended trot

This is the ultimate in gymnastic achievement at the trot and shows the maximum amount of thrust and impulsion that has been developed in the horse. It is a dressage gait and should only be used along the long sides or across the diagonals of the schooling arena, the horse being 'brought back' for the corners to be negotiated. This is important, as otherwise it will be in great danger of injury from overreaching. The extended trot is achieved by the great impulsion from the horse's quarters giving greater freedom to the shoulders, so the animal covers more ground with each stride, the strides being longer without becoming more lofty. This gait should not be attempted before the end of the second year's training or even later, for it makes exceedingly high demands on the horse's gymnastic ability that call for very great thrust and impulsion carried out with freedom and poise.

To begin, the rider employs a working trot which he modifies to something approaching a collected trot but with the horse's hind feet striking the ground in the tracks made by the forefeet. (In the truly collected trot the increased load taken by the hind feet will cause them to alight short of the forefeet tracks, the amount depending on the conformation of the horse.) Coming out of the corner into the long side of the schooling arena the rider uses increased driving controls to produce greater energetic thrust from the horse but at the same time does not allow the trot to become

For extended trot the rider uses increased driving controls to bring about greater energetic thrust; the horse must be allowed to extend its shoulders and neck. Only when advanced will the rider be able to remain seated at this gait.

hastier. The horse must be given the freedom to extend its shoulders and neck but should not be allowed to 'fall apart' or the timing and precision will degenerate and harmony will be lost, with overreaching a possible consequence. If the horse has the necessary strength and springiness as a result of its earlier training and can produce the extra vigour required, the extended trot will show the maximum amount of expression possible for that horse. The rider remains seated in the saddle for the collected trot, but he should rise for the extended trot. Only when horse and rider are at an advanced stage of training can the rider remain seated at the extended trot. When the pulsations of the horse's back are such as to make it easy to sit during the extended trot the trainer will know that the horse's natural ability has been completely developed.

Collected canter

Transitions to canter that have previously been obtained from the trot coming out of a corner of the school will now be asked for along the straight sides of the school, and as collection increases without loss of impulsion and mobility of the quarters a canter from walk can be performed. If the horse's transition to canter is faulty, if it evades an even loading on all four legs by turning its quarters to the inside, it should be brought back to a trot until supple collection is obtained before another transition to canter is tried. The rider should pay particular attention to ensure that his inside rein does not exert a backward pull, as this will cause the horse to evade the faulty control by turning its quarters out. It is worth spending time to correct faults at this stage, or the resulting faults of stiffness and crookedness will manifest themselves later and be difficult to eradicate.

Transition to canter from the trot will have been made in the early lessons, and after about a year of training transitions from walk to canter will have begun. This will be achieved when the horse's contact with the bit at the walk is positive enough and the reins can be shortened slightly. Many horses will leap into a canter when they are first asked to canter on in the confines of a schooling arena. This need not worry you during early training, but now the rider must insist on a calmer transition, with even loading on all four legs. Once this is mastered the shortened gait of the collected canter can be brought about without the gait losing its liveliness or beginning to drag. The rider's legs will cling to the horse's sides, and his seat will follow the elastic pulsations of the horse's back. To slow down the canter to the desired rate of collection the rider must withdraw his hands, supported by a deep driving and collecting seat, as the horse is in suspension with its head and neck at its highest point. This will ensure compliance from the horse's back so that subsequent light tugs in rhythm with the movement will load the quarters, shortening the length of leap but maintaining impulsion. As the horse slows down, the rider's legs act to sustain the leap of the hind legs, which are now more bent and engaging less far forwards, while his hands harmoniously release the leap. Eventually, only mere hints of the controls will be necessary, primarily tensing of the small of the rider's back. By this means the horse can be brought back to the walk and immediately cantered off again, with the opposite leg leading. The Spanish horse and rider are masters of this art of instant response to almost imperceptible controls. During this training, however, the transition to a working canter from a shortened working trot should not be neglected as an exercise for a smooth transition with the load evenly distributed on all four legs.

When asked for a transition from canter to walk the horse may at first put in a few trotting strides. If this is due to lack of strength in its joints the rider must not force it by the use of his controls. If, as will probably be the case with a horse that has progressed properly, it is due to the horse not understanding what is required, then calm repetitions on subsequent occasions will soon enable it to perform correctly. The collected canter will greatly improve the posture and suppleness of the horse, but again it must be emphasized that only clean, vigorous leaps with even loading on all four legs in the three-phase sequence already explained is acceptable. Lifeless gaits that drag, or a gathered-in gallop with four beats, are serious faults that must be corrected immediately by compelling the horse to leap forwards in a free canter of the correct three-beat timing.

When correct engagement of the hindquarters coupled with an active and elastic back is achieved, the rider will sit the horse gently and evenly not only at the collected canter but at the longer, freer canter also. If the rider's upper body has to rock forwards involuntarily at every leap of the canter it indicates that the horse's quarters are flying upwards because its joints are stiff and not yet fully loosened. If this happens, practise smooth transitions to canter from the walk, then halt after a few leaps before the haunches can stiffen. This will make the haunches more flexible and the fault will disappear. Trying to maintain a collected canter for too long will also cause the horse to seek a more comfortable position with haunches stiffened and unengaged. When the collected canter can be attained from the walk in the manner described, transitions can successfully be made from the free canter to the collected gait.

As assurance increases, the horse must be brought away from the support it draws from the outside line of the arena and worked through the middle, with the same precise attention to even loading on all four legs. It is also advisable to break up the routine by alternating work in the schooling arena with work in open country to avoid the horse becoming listless or unenthusiastic about its work.

Change of lead – flying changes

When the horse's dexterity has advanced to this stage, the rider can begin exercising for the change of lead at the canter. From a collected canter the horse is brought back to walk for a few steps; the rider adjusts his position and then asks for a transition to canter with the opposite lead. When this movement is completed smoothly the number of steps at the walk between each transition to canter with a changed lead can be diminished. This will eventually result in the rider bringing the horse back from collected canter to walk and then striking off immediately into canter again with the opposite lead. It is best to execute these changes along a straight line, at first along the long side of the school and then across the diagonal line from corner to corner. If the horse is of sufficiently high mettle, practising this movement will result in a transition from canter left to canter right and vice versa without any walking steps between; flying changes of lead will thus come automatically from the earlier exercise.

Horses and ponies not of the type for higher gymnastic movements should not be tormented with this type of exercise, and even those of sufficient verve should not be pushed into it too soon by over-zealous use of the controls backed up by spurs. A calm progression is needed so that the animal is not prejudiced against the movement but willingly accepts the new exercise. Changes of lead or flying changes at the canter occur at the moment of suspension after the third beat of the canter gait. The rider must therefore adjust his weight and leg controls and ask for the change to the opposite lead at the moment *before* the suspension phase of the gait. If he asks later than this (some advocate asking for the change of lead during suspension) it will be too late, as the hind leg propelling the first phase will have been 'committed' to grounding first, preventing the other hind leg from taking over. The horse may then change in front but not behind, producing a disunited canter. A disunited canter may also result if a short cut to the flying change is tried by cantering a tight figure of eight and suddenly trying to force a change on the curve. This is why it is best with a young horse to work on the change in straight lines. When large figures of eight are being used to improve collection, always prepare the horse and ask for the change of lead while moving across the centre of the arena. This will ensure that the horse changes and has time to settle to the correct lead well before it comes to the corner, and will not have to produce the much greater flexion that is required when changing from one circle to another. When teaching the movement, ask for the change at the same place along a straight line until the horse performs it willingly and calmly, but after that vary the point at which the change is performed; ride the horse over the same point without asking for a change of lead so that the controls are not anticipated. Always reward the animal when it has completed a successful change while it is learning, and revert the lesson back to less demanding work before the horse becomes tired of it. Any rushing, throwing about of the head or anticipating of the controls must be immediately overcome by bringing the animal back to a walk and then cantering on calmly to settle and quieten it. The rider's controls and the horse's response must eventually seem to be as one, carrying out the movement as a result of the same will.

Extended canter

This is developed from the medium canter. The whole framework of the horse extends, covering more ground but still maintaining the three beats and timing of the shorter gait. The forward leaps of the animal respond to the greater driving action applied by the

In the extended canter the rider goes along with the greater extension, using his seat to maintain the action and not falling forwards. The photograph shows the middle beat of the canter, with the inner hind and off fore grounded.

rider, who maintains a positive contact with the bit. The rider must go along with the greater extension and speed in order to maintain the action, but not fall forwards and lose his seat. The extended canter, like the extended trot, should only be ridden on straight lines, and with young horses the normal schooling arena will be too short for developing this gait properly. A large rectangle measuring approximately 60 metres along the long side is required, and the horse must then be brought to a medium canter by means of a half halt before the corner is reached.

Improving the walk

At the beginning of its training the young horse is allowed to walk freely with relaxed reins, and later contact with the bit is only maintained sufficiently to encourage the animal to reach forward into it. The trainer's concern at this stage is to ensure a forward walk, and he allows the young horse more rein if its steps become hurried or its stride shortens. As its poise and posture improve at the trot and canter more positive contact can be established, and after its first year of schooling a better walk with shortened reins results. Now, after a collection has been achieved at the trot and canter, we can begin work to produce a better walk. Producing a collected walk is left until this stage of training as it is one of the most difficult gaits the rider is called upon to produce from the horse and cannot be obtained truly until this later stage. There will always be greater opportunities for the horse to commit evasions at the walk (when the legs are grounded for longer periods) than at other gaits. The faults of a rider who naturally tends to give a greater precedence to his hand controls when combining them with his seat and legs will also have a more adverse effect at the walk than at other gaits, when they are partly cancelled by the increased impulsion. Another mistake is to ask for collection at the walk for too long a period, which will produce a defective gait. The animal must be given a chance to stretch and relax its muscles by allowing intervals of a free walk controlled by the rider's legs. When being trained at the walk, nervous horses of high mettle must be dissuaded from taking short, hasty steps by the rider's legs pliantly asking the animal to rediscover a relaxed, lengthened stride. For lazy horses the rider uses brief alternate taps of his legs to liven the gait, and reinforces this control with simultaneous use of the schooling whip behind his leg. However, this must not become a continuous alternating tapping on either side or dual tapping with the rider using both legs at once. If this were to happen the horse would become insensitive and unresponsive to the rider's leg controls. When the horse fails to respond, a brief, energetic pressure and a sharp reminder with the whip must teach the animal to obey the rider's driving leg control. Once this is achieved, the mere threat of the rider's leg produced by increased extension of his stretched calf muscles and the increased bracing of his back will be enough to produce the desired result.

Collected walk

With the horse responding freely at the walk the rider's legs must, like his hands, remain soft. Rough, kicking leg controls will disturb the horse, especially at the collected walk, when they will cause the animal to stiffen its back and hindquarters. The collected walk will start to develop from the ordinary walk as the hindquarters increase their engagement, allowing the forehand to become freer and higher with a corresonding upward extension of the neck from the withers. The centre of gravity moves towards the rear as the rider's driving control is applied, and a supple poll ensures a correct head carriage that only needs gentle support from the reins. The trainer will also observe the production of saliva as the horse chews or mouths the bit, and the relatively pronounced bending of the hind legs will cause them to make tracks behind those of the forelegs. Contact with the bit remains soft but positive throughout, as the shortened base of support and increased mobility is established.

Extended walk

This comes from the stages of the free walk producing long, relaxed strides, and from the collected walk, with increased hindquarter engagement resulting in the ability to extend. The horse is asked to walk forwards to seek contact with the bit, but not to hurry or lose its poise. The hind feet must now reach forward so that the tracks produced show ahead of those of the forefeet. When training the horse at the walk it is important to remember that this is the most difficult gait to improve from the animal's natural version. The trot can be very noticeably improved when starting from poor beginnings, but a horse that walks badly will show only marginal improvement. A horse's ability to take long strides in a free or extended walk, or to make lofty, expressive steps in the collected walk, is inborn and a result of the function of its joints by virtue of its conformation. If you are lucky enough to have a horse that possesses the required attributes you may, with patient and progressive training, be able to bring it to a state of mobility in the sequence of walking gaits that makes it a joy to ride and observe.

Rein back

I prefer to leave this part of the animal's training until the later stage for several reasons. In the first place, it is essential for the animal to attain full collection at the halt before a proper rein back can be done. Second, as the restraining controls are the same as the halt only stronger (in effect giving a continuation of the halt to the rear), the horse must have learned to move forward again at the slightest demand. If the horse's responsiveness is not up to these requirements, the rider will only manage to produce a hesitant movement not consistent with an alert response to both the backward and forward controls. Furthermore, if the horse learns prematurely that it can run backwards to escape the rider it will use this trick whenever it wants to disobey to avoid collection or otherwise to disregard the controls. Properly executed, the rein back is not a resentful, dragging movement but a schooling exercise that lowers the hindquarters and bends the joints of the haunches, ready to resume a smooth forward motion with unchanged posture at the slightest signal.

The controls given by the rider for a rein back are the same as he uses to start forward motion except that the reins act as a restraining force of sufficient intensity to make the lifted diagonals step backwards rather than forwards. After the required number of backward steps have been taken, the rider's pelvis produces the forward thrust to bring the horse to a halt with a fluid and immediate walk forwards. At the same time the hands are slightly relaxed, the degree depending on whether a halt or forward walk is

The rein back: positive backward steps with lowered hindquarters are controlled by the rider, whose pelvis must produce the forward thrust to activate a halt and immediate walk forwards.

being asked for. The rider's legs remain clinging to the horse's sides and his upper body remains vertical. If the horse creeps back with raised or lowered head, if its steps are broader or it moves to either side, it is not responding properly or the rider's controls are at fault. The fluent execution of this movement, with the rider able to control each step, is an infallible test of his driving and restraining controls and the harmony with which they are applied to his horse.

Turn on the haunches

To be performed correctly, this movement must be carried out in walked steps with no fewer than three legs always grounded. The centre of the turn is beneath the inner hind foot, which must remain in motion like the outside hind, and not merely turn on the spot. Begin by walking the horse along one side of the arena and almost into the corner. It is then brought to a halt but immediately asked for the turn on the haunches, so that it does not in fact come to a complete standstill. This will interrupt the forward walk enough to allow the change of direction to take place and bring the horse back on its haunches for the required degree of collection. At the moment before the halt, the rider uses both reins to lead the horse towards the inside; it describes a semicircle around its hindquarters with its hind legs stepping in place. Immediately the turn is completed, the horse is driven forwards again along the side of the school. The rider's outside shoulder moves forward as his pelvis activates the turn, and his upper body with its weight slightly to the rear follows the turn without being left behind. The rider's legs support the movement; his outside leg behind the girth initiates the turn by inward pressure to support the action of the reins, and his inside leg at the girth sustains the action of the

a *Turn on the haunches: the horse is brought back onto the haunches with its lightened forehand remaining in contact with the bit; the centre of gravity for the turn under the inner hind foot can be clearly seen as the horse begins stepping in an arc around its inner hind leg.*

b *Mid-way round, the horse is nicely balanced and in perfect contact with the bit with no sideways bending of the neck, falling inwards or rushing round.*

c *The inner hind leg, stepping in place, has maintained the centre of the turn and will now become the outer hind as the turn is completed and the horse moves off in the opposite direction.*

a

b

c

horse's hind legs and keeps the inner hind stepping in place. The reason for not going right into the corner of the school before starting the turn on the haunches is that the young horse will need to step forwards somewhat at the beginning of the turn until it learns to accept the increased burden on the hindquarters. This can be allowed to begin with, but the lightened forehand must remain in contact with the bit and the horse must not be allowed to bend its neck sideways and 'fall' inwards or rush round. The movement is essentially one of relaxed stepping, describing an arc around the inner hind leg. In later training the horse can be made to trot forwards as soon as the turn is completed. If this is done without hesitation, in the correct position and with poise, it can be assumed that the training has been correct and the gymnastic ability of the suppled hindquarters has been improved. Practice should be carried out with turns on the haunches in both directions, and the rider should always be able to get the horse to move straight forward at any given point of the turn.

⑨ Gymnastic training

Few people will be fortunate enough to work with a horse or pony that has an absolutely ideal conformation and temperament which will allow training to advance without difficulties. The more advanced training becomes, and the limit of the animal's ability is approached, the more these difficulties emerge. This must be borne in mind if the rider is not to suffer constant frustration and wear the horse out prematurely by trying to take it beyond its natural limits. The trainer's task is first to recognize the short-comings brought about by defects in the animal's conformation, which will present insuperable difficulties if training is advanced beyond a certain point. Second, he must distinguish between these insurmountable faults and those that by carefully adapted training can be eliminated or greatly improved. He will achieve success only if he can recognize the weak parts of the animal's body, gradually strengthen them by progressive exercise and in the meantime spare them from excessive loading.

The poorer the conformation, especially if muscle contour is lacking around the back, ribs and belly, the greater difficulty the horse will have in gymnastic efficiency. Animals with these faults require much more allowance for their shortcomings during training, as even when brought on slowly they will feel pain and discomfort that horses of more adequate conformation never experience. More frustrating, and more difficult to bring to willing obedience, are horses with the right strength and shape but that lack the spirit of animation so necessary for unconditional response to the rider's demands. The trainer's job here is to reawaken the animal's desire for work, and a no nonsense attitude at the very beginning, followed by gentle praise when free response has been given, will be needed. However, the truth of the old adage that defects of conformation are more easily overcome than defects of disposition will soon become apparent to any trainer.

Effective bitting

All types and shapes of bit, from the mild to the very strong, will be found in use throughout the world, with different countries tending to favour a particular type to apply various training methods. Generally speaking, the best bit for the young horse in its early training will be a thick, jointed snaffle, and it is important for anyone interested in training his own horse or pony to understand the reason for this. The action and objective of the different types of bit must be clearly understood. With the jointed snaffle the action on the animal's mouth is milder when the mouthpiece is thick, and can be applied to one side at a time to familiarize the young horse with what is intended. Also the force exerted is a 1:1 ratio between the rider's hands and the point of contact of the load. The centre joint, held on the tongue, also allows some of the applied force to 'escape' as it can swivel at the centre when pressure is applied.

A bit with a solid bar will act upon both sides of the lower jaw at once, even if it is being applied more strongly to one side than the other and the force is greater because it cannot 'give' in the middle. If it is connected to a side shank, the force exerted by the rider's hands will be multiplied many times as the length of the shank increases. (The impact of the force of bits with very long shanks is somewhat reduced in severity because as the length of the lever increases the force exerts itself more slowly.) These curb bits usually have chains that connect under the chin and intensify the lever action of the reins acting on the lower end of the shank.

The reason for using the mild jointed snaffle on young horses, therefore, is to teach them to accept the bit and go forwards into it, and not to be frightened by premature use of the extra lever action of the curb. The rider is also better able to teach the immature horse to obey the controls of the snaffle and have them willingly accepted when the pressure exerted by his hands on the animal's mouth has not been multiplied, as is the case when a curb is used. Once training has advanced to the stage where a degree of collection is obtained without loss of forward impulsion, familiarizing the horse with the action of the bar bit will do no harm. Unless the horse is of exceptional poise and mettle the fitting of a curb bit will not be desirable, however, until the horse has received two years of training from its initial schooling at four and a half years old. If hasty results are sought by using a curb before this, there is a real danger that instead of making the gait longer and more expressive the animal will lose its poise by opposing the lever action, and the gait will become dragging and expressionless. Even horses of the Spanish Riding School are often put back into snaffles and frequently trained in them to freshen and recondition their movements.

The benefit of a full double bridle can come only after the horse moves with impulsion and suppleness in collection, when the refinement of rein controls can be perfected. A steady, elastic contact with the horse's mouth can only be advanced to this degree by the use of lever action via the curb. When the double bridle is introduced the horse should be ridden in open country on straight lines, with the curb bit supported by the rider's hands but not operated. The curb chain is also left off at this stage. This will allow the horse gradually to reach for the bar bit and to accept it naturally, without resistance. When the curb chain is eventually fitted it must not be so loose as to irritate the horse by flapping when it is not in use. It should be fitted so that the top part of the bit, attached to the cheekpieces, can be drawn back to an angle of 45 degrees before pressure of the chain is felt on the chin groove. Only if patience is exercised before coming to the curb bit will the desired result be obtained. Then the load can be controlled as the lever action is applied, and this control will flow through the horse's neck, spinal column and haunches down to the pastern joints without being blocked on the way by resistance or false postures.

The rider, too, must be ready for the curb bit, and must be able to ride his horse with a supple and independent seat, always maintaining his balance, and with soft, steady hands that act in sympathy with the horse's mouth. Finally, the trainer must ensure the correct fitting of the curb bit so that the animal can chew comfortably and produce saliva. A horse will not respond correctly even to a well-fitting curb unless it has been suppled by the rider in its early training, but nor will a well-tuned horse move freely in an ill-fitting, uncomfortable bridle.

A bit I favour as an intermediate measure between the snaffle and a double bridle is the Kimblewick. It is not without its critics, some of whom claim it to be too severe. I do not agree with this, as long as all the points I have outlined are realized and the rider is of sufficient skill to use the bit intelligently. It is very good as a second stage bit for a young horse, and also for older horses that have been badly trained and will not willingly obey a snaffle. Horses used in harness that are to be retrained as saddle horses also resent the looser action of the jointed snaffle sometimes and prefer the firmer, even contact of the solid bar.

Advanced gymnastics

Few horses are capable of advancement to the ultimate gymnastic performance of *haute école* – the pure dressage of high school. Only those that have successfully completed two to three years of training and have clearly shown their rider that they are capable of high collection while maintaining good forward impulsion should

Gymnastic exercises for advanced horses: the author demonstrates a sitting, driving trot over poles to produce a lofty, energetic gait with a vigorous and elastic extension.

be asked to attempt the extra severity of this work. The increased bending of the haunches when collection is intensified will demand great effort from the muscles of the croup, which make the principal contribution and work exceedingly hard when lowering of the hindquarters is demanded. The flexor and extensor muscles of this region must be of such power that when trained to high school standard the horse can produce a gait that is lofty and energetic in collection and vigorous and elastic in the extended gaits requiring faster forward movement. No ordinary horse will be capable of this, nor should a utility horse be subjected to the torture of trying to have such movements 'squeezed' out of it. Having said that, there is no reason why an animal that has progressed satisfactorily cannot be asked for a few steps towards this goal, and any achievement should bring great joy to the rider when he feels quite clearly that the horse is performing with willingness and poise.

Collection at halt

A basic requirement will now be a greater degree of collection at the full halt, which can be turned into immediate forward engagement of the flexed hindquarters. To do this the horse must be brought to the halt still in positive contact with the bit and with its weight evenly distributed on all four legs. The horse must then respond immediately to the rider's controls by moving directly into a pure trot or into canter from the halt, with no intermediate steps. When this can be done with precision, it is proof that the horse's collection and response to the controls is of the highest degree. To pass directly from a standing start to a spirited canter will make fresh demands upon the animal's joints, and should only be attempted towards the end of the lesson when it is thoroughly warmed up but not fatigued. To execute a halt to canter transition the horse is first flexed, and then leg and seat controls are applied for a canter strike-off. This flexing will shorten the horse's base of support, causing the hocks to bend for the initial thrust-off and freeing the forehand for the chosen lead.

Half pass

Performed at the collected trot with poise and grace, this movement offers a captivating picture of harmony between horse and rider. The horse moves across the arena on two tracks, the forehand slightly leading the hindquarters, and with a slight bend

Half pass to the left: the rider's weight initially leads the movement and the horse steps across in unison with the rider's controls and the changing centre of gravity.

permitting the horse to look in the direction of the movement. The horse's outside shoulder must be freed by the slight inner bend of its body to allow the outer foreleg to step in front of the inner foreleg; the outer hind leg steps forwards and across the inner hind leg. No slowing of the pace can be allowed. The rider's weight must not merely follow the direction but initially lead the movement so the horse steps across where it is 'positioned', moving in unison with the changing centre of gravity.

To begin the half pass the horse is taken through the corner approaching the long side of the arena, but instead of the horse continuing down the long side the rider's outside leg presses its hindquarters towards the centre of the school. The pressure of the rider's outside leg coincides with the rising of the hind leg on that side. The rider's inside leg just behind the girth maintains the longitudinal flexion and collection, and ensures that impulsion is maintained. The inside rein keeps the horse facing in the right direction, and is shortened somewhat to correspond to the animal's flexion. The outside rein controls the longitudinal flexion of the neck and supports the lateral driving action of the rider's outside leg. The line taken is across the diagonal of the arena, the horse moving sideways nearly parallel to the long side. To begin with the half pass is only taken to the centre of the school, where the animal is allowed to go forwards in a straight line to the far end. Eventually the whole school can be crossed, and later a series of zigzags across a line down the centre of the arena can be added. It should be remembered that all two-track work is developed from the basic shoulder-in exercises, and these should be practised when difficulties arise.

Piaffe

The *piaffe*, often referred to as trotting on the spot, is not a trot as such but a movement executed in the phase sequence of the trot. It calls for a maximum flexion of the hindquarters to sustain the action, with the weight evenly distributed between the hind legs, which must step close together. This frees the forelegs from carrying almost any weight, allowing them to step loftily. The forearm is raised from the shoulder to a near-horizontal position; the forefoot is raised to a point between the middle of the cannon bone and the knee of the opposite foreleg, while the hind foot is raised only to about the level of the opposite fetlock because of the extra weight thrown upon the hind legs. The horse's back acts as a powerful spring to give the movement animated impulsion, the neck being raised with supple poll and a light but positive contact with the bit. Carried to the ultimate point of collection and weight transference to the lowered hindquarters, the rider will feel the horse almost ready to lift off completely in front to produce the

96

Teaching the piaffe *from the saddle: here the author uses the running rein to encourage greater collection and lowered haunches; the horse steps on the spot, with flexed hind legs stepping closer together.*

controlled rearing up of the *levade* should the controls be intensified.

Very few horses have the strength and ability to perform the *piaffe,* and those that can will do it with varying success. Even particularly gifted horses will need to advance slightly with each step during early training. There are several methods that are used to introduce the horse to the movement. At the Spanish Riding School horses are first worked in hand between pillars, and then with a rider helped by a trainer on the ground who works alongside and taps the horse's forelegs with a schooling whip to convey the desired lofty stepping. My own method, which I have adapted because I work from the saddle without the aid of anyone on the ground, is performed as follows. First I get the horse responding pliantly in a collected trot, and then I gradually intensify the restraining control of the reins while still exerting equal leg pressure with simultaneous taps in rhythm to the steps. As the horse slows down, I sustain the trot sequence and encourage the front steps to become loftier as I shift the centre of gravity to the rear, swinging my legs in time to the beat I wish the horse to maintain. When the horse gets the idea and responds with just one or two steps almost in place, I allow it to trot forwards again with words of praise and a gentle pat.

As training continues, the horse will begin to understand what is required and will perform more steps and carry its weight further backwards onto lowered haunches in order to elevate its forelegs. Do not try to obtain more steps than the animal can reasonably perform, as tensions and evasions will occur and the steps will become irregular, jerky and cramped with the hind legs not carrying the load elastically. The aim should be for both horse and rider to relax into the movement, which should be light and springy, and contact with the bit and the sides of the horse positive but light. When the movement ceases to be correct the horse must be energetically ridden forwards to take contact with the bit and restore a collected trot with positive steps. Later on, when a reasonable *piaffe* is coming fairly easily, the aid of an assistant to encourage the horse to perform loftier, more expressive steps can be useful. This will be done by gentle rhythmic taps on the back of the forelegs with a schooling whip, but not in such a way so as to frighten or over-excite the animal or the effect will be lost in tensions and hurried steps. The horse performing the *piaffe* properly will do it in a relaxed but expressive manner, and will be ready to move forwards again instantly this is signalled by the rider. Perfect *piaffe* is achieved only when the rising and grounding of the feet from bent haunches is soft and springy, without abrupt hopping, and with a supple body at maximum collection; the rider at all times in perfect harmony with the rhythm of the movement, without over-exertion, with relaxed hands and his buttocks not moving from the saddle.

Passage

This movement, also executed in the phase sequence of the trot, is similar to the *piaffe* in that the lowered hindquarters take over the weight, allowing the forehand to lift and become loftier through the pulsating of the horse's back. The two hind legs must again bear the weight equally, and produce the thrust to propel the animal forwards in what might be called a 'floating' trot. Because they are deeply bent, the hind legs are not raised much above fetlock level, while the 'released' front legs rise to the point where the forearm approaches the horizontal. The lifting of the forehand and contact with the bit are the same as in the *piaffe*. The same rules govern the movement, which must be performed straight and with correct timing and impulsion. It is also true that with the

Energetic passage: *the instant before diagonal thrust-off.*

piaffe and *passage* the amount of expression produced will vary from horse to horse even when performed correctly. Different breeds show different types of execution depending on their temperament and conformation. Horses of Spanish origin are usually especially good at these movements because their type of action, temperament and disposition suits advanced gymnastics of this nature, but even they will vary among individuals. Horses with shorter backs will also more easily support the weight on lowered haunches, and thus will be able to lift the forehand higher than those whose longer backs place the centre of gravity farther forward to begin with; animals with high quarters are also at a disadvantage. Any horse that is to perform the *piaffe* and *passage* well must be blessed with exceptionally strong joints, especially those of the pasterns and hocks.

There are varying opinions about the best methods of training for the *passage*. Some favour gradually allowing the horse to move forwards from a *piaffe*, while maintaining the timing and cadence, while others, of whom I am one, slow the tempo from a spirited collected trot by a gradual increase in collection. Most horses capable of a *passage* will respond to these methods if the rider is patient and does not force the issue by asking for too much too soon. The rider must be good enough to allow his seat to melt into the saddle, to initiate and maintain the rhythm, together with the almost imperceptible swinging of his legs and gentle squeezing of his hands. The rider's upper body remains upright, and the leg controls that produce the *passage* (and *piaffe*) are applied by simultaneous pressure on both sides not lasting for too long. A brief pressure from the rider's legs, exerting more energetic pressure when necessary, must produce a willing *passage* from the well trained horse, allowing the gait to be maintained by gently clinging legs and pliant seat and hand controls.

I should perhaps repeat, in conclusion, that the ability to perform movements at high school level on the part of the horse, and to ride them properly and teach them on the part of the rider, is rare. While they may represent the desired pinnacle of achievement for riders of exceptional horses, most horsemen and women should be well satisfied if they succeed in training their horses to become obedient and happy animals that work willingly and are a pleasure to ride.

10 Training aids and facilities

Special devices and pieces of equipment used in the training of horses and ponies cause much controversy as to the desirability of their use. Certainly there are no quick or easy gains to be made by the use of this or that gadget often advertised to cure certain problems or defects. Many of these devices are complicated, and if not used properly by a skilled operator can be injurious to the animal. For this reason many trainers express horror at the mere suggestion of their use, and claim that resorting to them is to admit defeat. This is generally true, and most horses and ponies will be better trained without the use of special devices. However, there are occasional problem horses that still persist with a fault despite all the normal schooling methods, applied with patience and skill. Where do we draw the line between 'normal' and 'special' equipment? All would agree that a lungeing cavesson, snaffle bridle and saddle are normal equipment necessary in the early training of the riding horse; most would accept side reins as normal for later lungeing, and also the use of special saddles, whip and spurs, together with a double bridle to improve outline, collection and performance in later training. What then of other types of bit, martingales, special bridles and other equipment used by many but looked upon with suspicion by some? In deciding if and when to use something other than the basic equipment in training the horse I believe the question one must first ask oneself is whether the animal has been given every chance with a rider and trainer of sufficient skill to bring it to its best, or is a device being used to overcome a fault in an animal whose basic training has been neglected. If the' latter is true, then the user is treating the symptom and not the disease. If this is the case, the horse will respond in a cramped, unsupple manner that will not produce the unconstrained impulsion and poise from which all correct movements develop. Before using any piece of extra equipment, therefore, the rider and trainer must be sure that enough sound basic training has been given, and that any faults or defects in the

101

horse are not the result of its being inadequately schooled or badly ridden.

Drop noseband guide

If you are confronted with a horse or pony that has been incorrectly schooled or badly ridden before coming to you, it may be necessary at first, if only for safety's sake, to use some form of restraining device, but this should be discarded as soon as possible in the retraining of the animal. If the animal has 'got away with it' for a long time, retraining to convert it into an obedient mount will need patience and skill. I have never found it necessary to resort to extreme measures in order to control a horse, but I have on occasions used a piece of special equipment to help me bring about a desired improvement. One simple little device that I devised, and call a drop noseband guide, helps to re-educate confirmed nose pokers or horses that because of earlier mistraining are stargazers. It can also be used successfully with former harness horses that will not drop their head when ridden. (It is sometimes also necessary with this latter group, whose muscles have 'set', first to use a draw rein in order to get the horse to bend correctly, but used incorrectly these can be injurious to the animal, and as they are very tiring they must be used for only brief periods.)

The muscles that shape the horse's outline must be gradually rebuilt in the form required for proper collection, but again I must stress that the rider must do this according to sound basic principles, only using any extra device to refine his controls. The drop noseband guide will help the rider to do this, and at the same time is mild enough to allow the horse to listen and respond to the rider's controls in the normal way. First tack the horse up with a snaffle and drop noseband, making sure it is fitted high enough on the nose to be well clear of the nostrils. This is very important. A strap is attached to the girth and brought between the front legs and up through a slot in a neck strap to hold it in place under the horse's neck. Where the strap from the girth passes through the neck strap a metal ring must be sewn on. The photographs show how all this is fitted. The only other item needed is a rubber strap with a hook on either end. These are in common use for car roof racks to hold camping equipment, suitcases, etc., and are sold at garages and hardware stores. They are usually covered with braided coloured nylon, and can be shortened by knotting the ends of the elastic that fit into the coiled part of the hooks on each end. When the horse is tacked up for a schooling lesson with the straps described, simply hook one end of the rubber to the drop noseband under the chin, pass it through the ring on the strap attached to the girth and then back to the drop noseband to form a loop. Again the photograph shows this clearly. The length of the

*With difficult horses a running rein can at first be used to encourage
correct head carriage, and then released leaving the rubber guide to
act on the drop noseband. It is particularly important to ensure that
the drop noseband is properly fitted round the bone of the nose to
avoid any possibility of the horse's breathing being impeded.*

rubber strap will depend on the size of the horse. It should be taut
when the animal holds its face perpendicular, stretched when the
face moves out, taking the nose in front of the perpendicular and
hang loose if the nose is held towards the chest in an over-collected
position.

With this little device the rider has complete control over his
mount; his hands are free to operate the reins acting on the snaffle,
while his seat and leg controls act normally to provide the required
impulsion. The horse is now schooled normally and asked for

103

The rubber guide used with a drop noseband acts on the animal's nose enabling the poll to remain high; it should be taut when the horse holds its face perpendicular.

collection, and whereas before it would lift its head, hollowing its back and poking its nose up, it now finds a gentle but progressive pressure on its nose asking it to lower its head. The rider can now produce impulsion with his legs and seat and with his hands softly encourage the correct head carriage. Another advantage of this device is that on bends and circles there is no uneven loading or sideways restriction, as the elastic guider acts under the neck and does not inhibit neck movement to either side. Only school for a short period, until the horse gets the idea and the impulsion being produced from the haunches can be felt moving freely through the animal's back, up to the poll and down to the bit. The device will not on its own produce a collected outline, nor should it, but it will greatly assist the rider to obtain the desired result. The strap must not be used for long periods or the horse will get so used to it that it merely 'leans' on it for support. When things are going well the rider can stop the horse, and by leaning forwards in the saddle simply unhook and remove the rubber strap. It can be replaced in the same way.

Always remember that no device or gadget can replace proper riding – when they are used to try and force the horse into a movement they can often be harmful. Their only benefit is in helping the horse to understand more clearly what it is being asked to do.

Draw reins and running reins

Where these need to be used I advise a method based on the principle I devised for the rubber guide. This is to fasten one end of the draw/running rein to the ring under the neck on the animal's chest, pass it through the ring of the bit – in to out – then up to the rider's hands and back through the ring of the bit on the other side and back to the ring under the neck. The reason I prefer this to the normal draw rein arrangement is because it eliminates the chance of the horse getting its leg through the draw rein. This can easily happen with a low fastened draw rein when things go wrong, and the resulting entanglement is very dangerous. (I have even seen

Running reins: even with 'soft' hands (note the 'open' fingers) it is still easy to overbend the horse; here the head and poll are lowered slightly too much, though the horse is still stepping forwards into the bridle.

professional trainers using this method for jumping – a very dangerous practice in my view.) Using my system, with the rein attachment higher up on the chest, this danger is eliminated. There is another advantage: the pull of the rein acts on the horse's nose, and it therefore tends to respond without over-lowering its neck, whereas when the attachment point is at the girth it tends to pull the whole neck down.

Outdoor schooling arenas

Anyone wanting to train a horse or pony seriously will need a level, rectangular area for schooling work to be performed. This may be provided by a local riding and training establishment, while those who live too far from such centres will try to make do with a corner of a field. The problem with this is that in most countries it is unusable in winter because of wet or freezing weather. Mud or frozen earth is no surface for producing precise collected movements, and hard-baked summer surfaces also give rise to problems. For those with enough land – and money – the answer is to have a schooling arena of their own that can be used in all weathers. These are of course expensive to build, but by doing the work oneself the cost can be halved. Various materials can be used to provide an all-weather outdoor surface – sand, peat, wood bark, shavings or wood fibre. Anyone planning to build his own schooling arena will be limited by what is available and the cost; there are several pitfalls to be avoided whatever material is used. I studied the problems before building my own all-weather area, and I will deal step by step with the procedure based on this experience.

Site

In my opinion it is of little use to build a schooling arena of less than the standard 20 by 40 metres. Proper training will be very difficult to achieve in an area much smaller than this and any jumping other than small cavalletti will be almost impossible. When there is additional space, building smaller will always result in regrets that a larger area was not constructed.

Siting is very important. Never choose a hollow or anywhere natural drainage is bad or you will have problems in wet weather. If you have the choice of a site either sheltered by trees or in the open, remember that trees can blot out winter sun whereas an open site might provide the horse with too much opportunity to look around and be distracted by things of interest, and so not pay attention. My site is high up, open to the sun to east and south with a high bank to the west and trees along the north side. My horses do tend to look at the view along one long side, but I had no choice and it is nice and sunny all year whenever the sun is shining. When

I wanted to build the schooling arena the only piece of land available was a very sloping field. After many hours studying all the angles and gradients, I finally decided to have the length of the rectangle dug out across the slope and the excavated earth pushed to the lower side, building it up to form the other half of a level rectangle. This left the high bank along the top long side and a steep drop away along the other. The work took three days with a digger, and the site was then left to settle for the winter. About 3 ft (1 m) of earth was needed in the spring to build up the settlement; this had been foreseen, and a large dump of earth had been left to use at this stage. After levelling up again, the site was left for a further six months, and then finished when the digger dug out for the drains. A word of warning about banks. Never leave them at an angle of more than 45 degrees, as they will almost certainly slip. Mine were too steep; rain and frost caused them to slip after the arena was finished, giving me the problem of removing mud from the top of the all-weather surface. I then had to reinforce the banks with sunken iron stakes to help contain them, a very difficult task after the work had been completed.

Drainage

This is the most important single factor, and must be got right first time. If you get it wrong and have laid your top surface all your money and effort will have been wasted. The site must first be cleared and levelled to leave a 9 in (23 cm) fall across the rectangle from one long side to the other. For a 20 by 40 metre arena (all the figures will be based on this) four rows of 4 in (10 cm) land drains should be laid across the fall to pick up a 6 in (15 cm) drain along the lower perimeter that leads away to a suitable drainage point. Put the drains about 1 ft (30 cm) deep and fill in above them with stone. With a difficult site where natural drainage is not good a 6 in (15 cm) drain around the whole perimeter will be desirable. My own site had a small stream running through the centre of it, and this was diverted into a 9 in (23 cm) drain right under the arena to a point some 12 ft (4 m) below at the bottom of the lower bank.

Containing the perimeter

With the site levelled and the drains installed you must now contain what will be the finished arena, which must come within your perimeter drain. Availability and cost will again determine the choice of materials, but by far the best way to contain the arena is with good quality second-hand railway timbers laid edgeways on concrete blocks. I used the larger 12 in by 6 in (30 cm by 15 cm) type, each about 12 ft (4 m) long, and laid them lengthways on their narrow edge supported by 6 in (15 cm) concrete blocks laid flat. The blocks are placed at the correct intervals to form a 20 by

40 m rectangle, and the timbers are laid end to end on top of them to make an enclosed area 18 in (45 cm) high. Where each timber butts up to the next, drive a spike into the ground on the outside of the rectangle and pin it to the timber to hold it in position. Old ex-army steel bed frames cut into suitable lengths are ideal for this but make sure that no sharp edges are left exposed where a horse could tread on them or skin its leg. At the part of the rectangle intended for the entrance leave the timbers unsecured so that a lorry can get in. Next the whole area needs to be covered with stone to a depth of 6 in (15 cm), bringing it up to the level of the bottom of the timbers around the sides. Some people use 4 in (10 cm) of large stone and then fill on top with 2 in (5 cm) of fine stone so it can be rolled smooth, but I do not favour this as it tends to seal the surface and make it less easy for water to soak through. I used broken stone of 3–4 in (7–10 cm) diameter so it was more 'open', and rolled this as flat as possible; it works perfectly. The stone must be packed under the raised timber surround and extend outside for about 6 in (15 cm).

Separator

Once the stone is in position and rolled level, a liner must be laid over it to act as a separator between the stone and the final infill material. This is vital, as without it the stones will work up to the surface and the top material will pack into the stone beneath and cause poor drainage. The liner is made of thin, very tough glass fibre blanket, and comes in rolls about 8 ft (2.5 m) wide. In the UK it is called Polyfelt TS, and is used during the construction of major highways. It allows water to pass through it and does not rot. It is rolled out across the rectangle from one long side to the other. Each strip must overlap 9 in (23 cm), and each end should be nailed to the surrounding timbers with lengths of batten. It is then necessary to join the overlapped edges by what is called melt-joining. One person lifts the overlapped edge and applies heat along the underneath with a blowlamp or bunsen burner until the liner changes colour from white to brown. A second person seals the overlapping edge by walking along it to press it down. The flame of the burner must not be too concentrated or fierce as the material melts very quickly and it is easy to burn large holes right through the blanket. It is also best to choose a still day for this operation, as windy conditions cause heating problems with the flame and the material blows about when it is lifted; for successful bonding the day must also be dry.

Final infill

The choice of material to provide the working surface will to some extent depend on availability, as much of the cost will be for

108

Preparing the site for an all-weather arena: the rectangle is formed by railway timbers laid on concrete blocks (see arrow).

Sufficient stone to fill up to the lower edge of the timber surround is necessary (see arrows).

Tipping lorries run back over the final infill fibre to prevent damage to the separator (top arrow). *The overlapped joints of the separator can be seen* (bottom arrow).

transport. I do not recommend sand except in hot, dry climates, as it becomes heavy in the wet and also freezes. Wood shavings are too loose to provide a good footing for the animal, and pulverized bark is also less good than the material I favour, which is specially manufactured wood fibre. It is widely advertised by different firms, and delivery is arranged by lorries each carrying 30 to 50 cubic metres. It will require some 66 tonnes (approximately 200 cu. m) to fill the area to a depth of 9 in (23 cm). The lorries must be able to back up to the site and will then tip and run back over the material so as not to rut the stone base or damage the polyfelt. When all the material has been dumped in lumps over the rectangle, it can be spread by hand using a large rake. It is very light and spreads easily. The final task is to roll the arena, and this can be done with a tractor and 6 ft (2 m) roller or by hiring a vibrating roller. As the material compacts down to about 6 in (15 cm), all that is necessary for maintenance is to rake it level from time to time.

An all-weather surface properly constructed in this manner should give many years of trouble-free use and will prove to be of immeasurable value.

Index

Aids 13
Arenas, construction of 106–10

Back, elastic 41, 82
  hollow 25, 44, 104
  horses 61, 69
  muscles 36
  pulsating 79, 81
  stiff 44, 78, 86
Balance 11, 12, 14, 25, 26, 36, 61, 69, 93
Bit, contact with the 62, 77, 79, 81, 84–6, 93
  finding the 37, 38, 77
  leaning on the 79
Bitting 92, 93, 102–5
Breaking out 62

Canter 64–6, 95
  collected 81
  disunited 83
  extended 84
Cavalletti 68, 74
Cavesson, lungeing 45, 46
Centre of gravity 78, 95, 96, 99
Change of lead 83, 84
Circles at the trot 57–9
Collection 43, 62, 76–8, 81, 87, 93–6, 99, 102, 104
Commands 47
Conformation 17–23, 76, 80, 86, 91, 98
Controls 14, 77, 85, 103, 104
  diagonal 58
  driving 14, 38, 66, 70, 77, 80, 84, 85, 88
  lateral 58
  refining of the 102
  restraining 14, 87, 88, 97
Coordination, legs and seat 38, 39, 99, 100
Crookedness 43, 61, 81

Draw reins 105, 106
Driving force 32
Drop noseband 102
  guide 102

Early training 16, 17
Equilibrium 14
Evasions 43, 59, 85, 98
Exercises, rider's 9–11

Flexion 58, 96
Flying changes 83, 84
Foot position, rider's 33, 34
Forward reach 36, 77

Gait 14, 40, 41, 44, 59, 62, 77, 79, 80, 82, 85, 86, 92, 100
Gymnastic movements 83, 84
  training 91–3

Half halts 57, 85
Half pass 95, 96
Hands, influence of the 14, 15, 27, 28, 38, 41, 61, 77, 78, 82, 103
Haute école 93
Head, carriage 86, 102–5
  horse's 77
  poking 102, 104
  rider's 61
  shaking 43, 84
Hind legs, dragging 36, 40, 62, 77, 78
Hindquarters, lowering of the 76, 78, 87, 94, 98
  strengthening of the 57
Hocks 61

Impulsion 36, 59–61, 70, 77–80, 82, 85, 93, 96, 98, 101, 103, 104
Independent seat 38, 93

Joints 17, 61, 64, 67, 78, 82, 87, 95, 99
Jumping 67–75
Jumps, practice 74, 75

Knee, rider's 30, 31, 73
  position 9, 69, 73

Lateral flexion 58
Learning to ride 11, 12
Legs, the rider's 32–4, 61, 70, 77, 82
Leg yielding 61
Ligaments 17, 35, 64, 67
Longitudinal flexion 96
Long reining 52–4
Lungeing 45–51

Older riders 11, 12, 23, 33
Outline 78, 102–6
Overreaching 62, 67, 80, 81

Pace 14
Passage 98–100
Pasterns 25
Pelvis, the rider's 8, 9, 66, 87, 88
Piaffe 28, 29, 96–8
Poise 59, 77, 78, 80, 85, 86, 90, 92, 94, 95, 101

Rein back 86, 87
Riding position 9, 38
Rising trot 59
Running reins 105, 106

Saliva, producing 38, 77, 86, 93
Schooling arenas, all-weather 106–10
Seat, deep 8, 9
   driving 81
   forward 29, 30, 70
   jumping 29, 30, 33, 69, 70
   loose 30, 85
   normal 13, 25, 38, 40
   types of 29–31
Selection 17, 18
Serpentines 57
Shoulder-in 61, 63
Side reins 50, 51
Small of the back 13, 38, 61, 66, 82

Stiffness, rider's 28, 29
Stirrup lengths 30, 31, 33

Temperament 98
Tendons 35
Thrust 36, 60, 61, 79, 80, 95, 98
Tracking up 36, 37
Training aids 101–6
Training facilities 101, 106–10
Transitions 41, 81, 82
Trot, collected 78, 97, 99
   extended 79–81
   working 40, 78
Trotting poles 68
Turn on the forehand 55–7
Turn on the haunches 88–90
Two tracks, working on 61

Upper body 14, 26, 27, 82

Verve 17, 83
Voice 47

Waist, the 13, 14
Walk, the 85, 86

Young horse, the 16, 17, 85